The Care of Souls

The Care of Souls

Reflections on the Art of Pastoral Supervision

LOGAN C. JONES

Foreword by Wayne L. Menking

WIPF & STOCK · Eugene, Oregon

THE CARE OF SOULS
Reflections on the Art of Pastoral Supervision

Copyright © 2019 Logan C. Jones. All rights reserved. Except for brief quotations in critical publications or reviews, no part of this book may be reproduced in any manner without prior written permission from the publisher. Write: Permissions, Wipf and Stock Publishers, 199 W. 8th Ave., Suite 3, Eugene, OR 97401.

Wipf & Stock
An Imprint of Wipf and Stock Publishers
199 W. 8th Ave., Suite 3
Eugene, OR 97401

www.wipfandstock.com

PAPERBACK ISBN: 978-1-5326-7304-7
HARDCOVER ISBN: 978-1-5326-7305-4
EBOOK ISBN: 978-1-5326-7306-1

Manufactured in the U.S.A.   MARCH 27, 2019

To My Parents

In Memoriam

I suppose that trying to put his pain into words was the story of his life. Maybe it is the story of all our lives.

FREDERICK BUECHNER

The paradox of learning a really new competence is this: that a student cannot at first understand what he needs to learn, can learn it only by educating himself, and can educate himself only by beginning to do what he does not yet understand.

DONALD SCHÖN

Contents

List of Illustrations | ix
Foreword by Wayne L. Menking | xi
Preface | xv
Acknowledgements | xix

1 The Psalms of Lament and the Transformation of Sorrow | 1
2 Silent Night | 19
3 The Clinical Rhombus Revisited: Learning Through Resistance and Change | 22
4 A Teachable Moment—For the Both of Us | 36
5 Descent into the Underworld: The Hero's Journey as a Model for Group Development | 38
6 A Prayer for Healing Denied | 48
7 You Learn It in Your Heart: Transformative Learning and Clinical Pastoral Education | 50
8 A Psalmist | 65
9 PFM as a Standard of Practice | 67
10 Men's Movement | 69
11 I Walk Through Life Oddly: Dispositions, Character, and Identity in Clinical Pastoral Supervision | 72
12 Symbols and Certification | 86
13 The Arc of Imagination in Transformative Learning Theory | 89
14 The Dream and the Gift | 101

Bibliography | 103

List of Illustrations

Orientation—Disorientation—New Orientation Schema | 7

The Clinical Rhombus | 23

The Clinical Rhombus Revisited | 24

Foreword

ANYONE WHO KNOWS LOGAN Jones or has been familiar with his writing and work as an ACPE clinical educator (formerly known as CPE supervisor) will know the extent to which he hears and attends to the depths of the soul—his, his students, and the recipients of his care. At the same time, they will also know that Jones does not practice his craft of soul care and clinical teaching without sound theological and theoretical foundations. What follows in this book will not disappoint you! Alternating rich and powerful stories from his own pastoral and teaching experience with thoughtful reflection on a myriad of theoretical material, Jones makes clear that care for the soul *and the teaching of care for the soul* are a balanced blend of risky—and often painful—exploration into the depths of one's own soul *and* thoughtful reflection on the theological and theoretical foundations that undergird our practice.

It is not insignificant or coincidental that Jones begins his work with a reflection on the lament Psalms and their importance for the work of soul care! Using Brueggemann's scheme of orientation, disorientation, and new orientation, along with the work of other notable biblical scholars, Jones makes the compelling theological case that the parallel processes of providing soul care and teaching soul care require the student and the teacher to engage their own movement from what is safe and secure to what will feel dangerous and unknown as they encounter the grief and pain that comes with this work. It cannot be otherwise. At the same time, he boldly holds forth the promise—as do the Psalms—that when this engagement is authentic and real, the mysterious presence of the Holy will be discovered in new ways, and unexpected learning will occur for both the student and the teacher. As Jones says, "Learning about one's own laments is not for the faint of heart. It requires a movement down into the depths. It calls for a bold act of faith which is new and maybe even radical. Such learning runs counter to our cultural expectation that we somehow "move on" when faced with pain and sorrow. Such learning requires the subversive acts of active listening, attending to the pain, giving voice to the voiceless."

But Jones is clear that attentiveness to one's laments and the laments of others is not about self-pity or being victimized by the suffering of the soul. There is a difference between hearing and attending to its pain and staying stuck in it. Transformative learning can only occur when the truths of what have long been denied and conveniently kept undercover are courageously engaged. Transformative learning is more than cognitive change: it is a change of heart! And might we dare say, it is a *metanoia and salvation* experience, to which many who have experienced clinical pastoral education will testify!

Jones is an artist. He is a creative and imaginative writer. Like the painter or musician, he has a deep perception of what lurks in the depths of our human experience, as well as an awareness of the mysterious presence of God hidden in those experiences. In artful words and language, he brings them to life in a way that will open the reader (myself included!) to new and deeper reflections on one's human experience and suffering and the power that is hidden therein.

I think what follows will be a very helpful read for the student who is experiencing clinical pastoral education for the first time. It will remind the beginning student—and the student who is in a second-year residency—that the experiences of helplessness at a bedside and not knowing what to say or do are not only a normal part of learning. They are experiences that are common to the teacher and the "expert." You are not alone! This book will

Foreword

also give you hope and courage to engage your disorientation, the moment you recognize that everything you expected soul care to be turns out not to be the case, the moment you recognize that you can't fix anything, and the moment you begin wondering if you have any ability at all. Well, you do, but it will take the experience of disorientation to recognize that your abilities may not be what you thought. At the same time, it will be a reminder that learning to be a skilled and artful worker of soul care will require your affective and emotional work to be integrated and balanced with foundational theology (or its equivalent in your faith tradition) and theory. This book will also be a good and helpful read for the seasoned clinical educator. It will serve as a reminder of why you do what you do and remind you to pay attention to the deep soulful experiences that brought you here and the theological and theoretical foundations through which you frame your work.

Using the richness of his own human experience—and dream life—along with deep biblical and theological underpinnings, Jones reminds us that the artful practice of soul care and the artful practice of teaching soul care are still wrapped up in being able to receive and offer blessings, and that all of our messy, bumbling, and painful journeys towards maturity are never final or fully complete, yet somehow they are always mysteriously blessed with a holy and sacred presence. He is attuned to this presence and he honors it—in himself, in his students, and in the persons who receive his soul care. While Jones does not offer new educational theories or theological revelations, his artful way of integrating theology, theory, and experience will awaken and enliven what is inside of you and what you already know! I am enormously grateful for his work and for offering himself to us in the way that he has! And I am grateful that he is a colleague in the work and teaching of soul care.

Dr. Wayne L. Menking
ACPE Certified Educator
Fort Worth, Texas
The Season of Epiphany, 2019

Preface

THESE ESSAYS AND SHORT reflections provide a window into my journey in becoming a chaplain and an ACPE supervisor (now called an ACPE certified educator). Over the years, writing has been a way for me to gain clarity of my feelings, to gather a better sense of theoretical understanding, and more importantly, to know more about myself. In this journey, I found there is no easy way to learn the art of pastoral care because it involves learning about oneself, one's soul. There are no shortcuts. As Donald Schön suggests, a person has to begin to do exactly what he or she does not know how to do. This means the learning process is often messy and chaotic, full of bitter resistance. It can be terrifying as well as exhilarating and life-giving. In my learning process, I was often well-defended and resistant to any feedback; some things were too painful to take in and hear. Other times, flashes of insight would come and my sense of calling reverberated within, letting me know I was on my right path. Learning, in the CPE process at its best, is transformative. It is soul-making.

Learning from the living human document means learning to listen to the narrative—both to what is spoken and what is left unspoken. The narrative lies at the heart of the pastoral care encounter. Listening requires patience. It requires a certain sense of humble quietness and giving up the need to respond with an answer or solution. Listening does not mean fixing. Listening means being as fully present to the other person as much as one is able. It is much harder than it sounds. It is the essence of what we do and who we are as CPE supervisors. Teaching, for me, means knowing my story so that I might be able to listen to the story of the other.

Being a chaplain in the acute-care hospital setting is not for the faint of heart. Pain lurks around every corner. There is rawness at the bedside. We see persons at their most vulnerable, in their grief and sorrow. We also see persons at their best. We experience their resiliency, their love for their families, and their deep hope. Healing happens when persons are able to put their pain into words, as Frederick Buechner so eloquently says, and into stories. Healing also occurs when love and care are gathered into words and stories.

The short reflections are my musings about some of my many failures in trying to provide pastoral care and my feelings of helplessness at the bedside. There are also narratives of my learning about the process of pastoral supervision. How many times did I learn I could not fix another person's pain? How many times did I wish I had a how-to manual that would tell me what to say, what to do, and who to be? The essays reflect my attempts to make sense and meaning of the supervisory encounters. So here are different aspects of supervisory theory coupled with musings on the implications for pastoral care: the Psalms of lament, the clinical rhombus, group process theory, transformative learning theory, and the importance of dispositions, character, and identity in pastoral supervision. It is my hope that the readers of this collection—CPE supervisors, CPE students, seminary students, and others—will get a glimpse of the many facets of pastoral care and supervision, such as the importance of self-awareness, the inexact art of caring, and the hard necessity of listening to pain.

I am deeply grateful to those who supervised me in this process. I thank Jenny Guffey, who supervised my first unit of CPE at Duke University Medical Center; Nape Baker, Wayne Robinson, and Perry Miller in my first-year residency at North Carolina Memorial Hospital in Chapel Hill; and John Detwiler and Dick Goodling in my second-year residency at Duke. I especially thank David Franzen and Peter Keese who supervised me in the supervisory CPE program at Duke. They all challenged and cared for me in untold ways. They believed in me when I could not believe in myself. I count myself blessed to have learned from each of them. I count them as mentors and friends.

While names and circumstances have been changed to protect privacy, I thank the many patients and families who allowed me to walk with them in the hard, sacred moments of life. I hold them in my heart. I also thank the many unnamed students who, over the years, allowed me to learn with them as their supervisor. Their courage to do this work, their trust in me with their pain, and their willingness to learn about themselves and their life narratives humble me. They taught me what it means to be a CPE supervisor. Their impact on me is profound. However, any shortcomings in these articles and reflections are mine alone.

I thank my colleagues: Carole Somers-Clark, Nancy Osborne, Charla Littell, and now Gyasi Patterson, Jeremy Gilmore, and Carolyn Remaklus. I am grateful for their friendship, their passion for this work, and their patience with me. It has been fun.

I especially thank my wife, Kelli, and my daughters, Sarah and Kate. With their love, wisdom, and laughter, my world is full beyond measure.

Finally, this book is dedicated in memoriam to my parents. They gave me the freedom to find my way into my calling. They cared for my soul.

Acknowledgements

I THANK THE EDITORS of the following journals in which earlier versions of these articles and reflections previously appeared.

The Journal of Pastoral Care & Counseling (formerly *The Journal of Pastoral Care)*: "The Clinical Rhombus Revisited"; "The Psalms of Lament and the Transformation of Sorrow"; "Silent Night"; "You Learn It in Your Heart: Transformative Learning Theory and Clinical Pastoral Education"; "Men's Movement"; "The Dream and the Gift"; and "A Prayer for Healing Denied."

Plainviews: "PFM as a Standard of Care."

Reflective Practice: Formation and Supervision in Ministry (formerly *The Journal of Supervision and Training in Ministry)*: "A Psalmist"; "Descent into the Underworld: The Hero's Journey as a Model of Group Development"; "A Teachable Moment—For the Both of Us"; "Symbols and Certification"; "I Walk Through Life Oddly: Dispositions, Character, and Identity in Clinical Pastoral Education"; and "The Arc of Imagination in Transformative Learning Theory."

I

The Psalms of Lament and the Transformation of Sorrow

In her book, *The Cloister Walk*, poet Kathleen Norris quotes a Benedictine monk as saying, "God behaves in the psalms in ways he is not allowed to behave in systematic theology."[1] The Psalms are different. They speak to life in ways other Scripture, doctrine, and theological presuppositions are not able to. The Psalms are poetry. As such, they offer a different view of life. The Psalms offer a view of life that is thick, rich, and runneth over. They seek not so much to explain but to offer the reality of life lived in all its messiness, both the pain and praise. Norris puts it this way, ". . . poetry's function is not to explain but to offer images and stories that resonate with our lives."[2] The Psalms capture the height, the depth, and the breadth of life lived in relationship to and in covenant with God.

In the life of faith, the Psalms are not simply an outlet for devotional prayers or "pious thoughts," as Roland Murphy says.[3] The Psalms are about honest dialogue with God. In this dialogue, nothing is held back. It is raw, down and dirty. The spoken words

---

1. Norris, *Cloister Walk*, 91.
2. Norris, *Cloister Walk*, 95.
3. Murphy, "Faith of the Psalmist," 235.

are evocative. They are relentless. To this end, they are true. The words of the Psalms speak to the very core of human experience in ways other language cannot begin to approach. In this way, the Psalms teach us how to pray. The Psalms teach us how to stand faithfully before God, asking and even demanding response, action, and answers. The Psalms teach us to bring our hopes, praise, and joy to God. They also teach us to bring our fear, pain, and sorrow.

This paper will explore how the psalms of lament can be a resource for pastoral care, how they can provide depth and meaning in times of grief, and how ultimately they can transform sorrow. The primary point will be that the psalms of lament do not dismiss or deny or seek to avoid sorrow. On the contrary, they allow a grieving person to move more fully into the valley of the shadow, knowing on different levels that no matter what, God is indeed present in the sorrow. I will provide a brief overview of the psalms of lament, paying particular attention to Walter Brueggemann's schema of orientation—disorientation—new orientation as a way of understanding the laments.[4] The implications of using the psalms of lament as a resource for pastoral care will be noted as it relates to the theological learning of seminary students who are participating in a Clinical Pastoral Education (CPE) program.

The Psalms of Lament

The scholarly consensus on the Psalms, and particularly the laments, suggests that a distinctive movement from plea to praise characterizes the lament psalm.[5] This movement may be sharp and somewhat disjointed at times. It may be uneven. Nevertheless, this movement from plea to praise is essential in understanding the power of the psalms of lament. Moreover, the current scholarship

---

4. Brueggeman, *Message of the Psalms*; Brueggemann, *Praying the Psalms*; Brueggemann, "Psalms and the Life of Faith," 3–32; and Brueggemann, *Spirituality of the Psalms*.

5. Mowinckel, *Psalms in Israel's Worship*; Gunkel, *Psalms*; and Westermann, *Praise and Lament*.

The Psalms of Lament and the Transformation of Sorrow

of J. David Pleins, Michael Jinkins, and Denise Dombkowski Hopkins supports this consensus.[6]

For Westermann, this movement from plea to praise is the movement of faith in God. The movement ranges from deep alienation and pain to profound trust, confidence, and gratitude. The recognition of this movement is central to Westermann's understanding of the Psalms.[7] This movement of faith does not shy away from the reality of brokenness and grief. They are certainly acknowledged and named. The reality of brokenness and grief is not denied in the laments. But—and this "but" is a critical aspect of the movement—the movement does not stay stuck in the plea, in brokenness and grief. There is more beyond. There is ultimately praise. There is an unparalleled transformation of sorrow into something more, call it praise, joy, wisdom, hope. Murphy describes this movement which ends in praise like this: "It is as though Israel could never give up on the Lord; an ineradicable strain of hope and expectancy surrounds the lament."[8]

Generally speaking, the lament is a stylized form of speech. It is a cry of distress. It is a protest or a complaint that seeks, and certainly expects, a positive outcome from God, that God deliver, that God save, that God show compassion upon the one who cries out. Throughout its history, Israel knew that along with the joy and blessing of life come, as Brueggemann says, "hurt, betrayal, loneliness, disease, threat, anxiety, bewilderment, anger, hatred, and anguish."[9] That is our history as well. Nothing has changed. We too know that life is not always good and happy. Bad things happen. The lament gives expression to the kinds of experiences and feelings we are told—constantly and relentlessly by our culture—to suppress.

But by praying the laments, Israel had a way of directly facing the hurtful dimensions of human life. Israel did not try to explain them away, deny them, or avoid them. Instead, Israel held

---

6. Pleins, *Psalms*; Jinkins, *In the House*; and Dombkowski Hopkins, *Journey*.
7. Westermann, *Praise and Lament*.
8. Murphy, "Faith of the Psalmist," 236.
9. Brueggemann, "From Hurt to Joy," 67.

to the premise that all of life—even the hurtful dimensions—was embraced by its covenantal relationship with God. The lament enables Israel to stay engaged and in dialogue with God. The lament affirms that even though there is pain in the world, this pain can be put into words. Brueggemann puts it like this:

> The laments show clearly that biblical faith, as it faces life fully, is uncompromisingly and unembarrassedly dialogic. Israel . . . in their hurt have to do with God, and God has to do with them. The laments are addressed to someone. Nowhere but with God does Israel vent its greatest doubt, its bitterest resentments, its deepest rage. Israel knows that one need not fake it or be polite and pretend in the divine presence, nor need one face the hurts alone.[10]

At its core, the lament is witness to a profound faith that takes God seriously and takes the covenantal relationship with God seriously. This means there has to be dialogue. There has to be exchange in open and honest ways. There can be no holding back. Everything is on the table: doubt, anger, despair, guilt, resentment. There is no requirement of politeness. There is no need for gentility. If the relationship is authentic, then it can endure and even thrive on the honest and candid expression of all of the hurtful feelings. These feelings have to be spoken in order for them to be dealt with. Silence in the face of hurt does no good. The anguish of life calls for speech, for words, for prayer. The anguish of life calls for poetry.

For Israel, the lament was the characteristic way of expressing and voicing the hurt of life. The Book of Psalms attests to this fact in a concrete way. More than one third to one half of the Psalms are laments.[11] Clearly in its life of faith, Israel is unafraid to speak its truth about the hurts found in that life. In its bold faith, Israel addresses God in its need and goes beyond. Israel asks and even demands that God should respond decisively to alleviate the spoken need. Israel even goes beyond in praying that God should

---

10. Brueggemann, "From Hurt to Joy," 68.
11. Brueggemann, *Reverberations of Faith*.

The Psalms of Lament and the Transformation of Sorrow

respond. Israel prays that God must respond. There is no other option.

As stylized speech, Israel developed a disciplined form for the lament. The form, and the words embodied in the form, worked then. It still works. As Brueggemann says, "The community uses, reuses, and rereuses these same words because the words are known to be adequate and because we know no better words to utter."[12]

The lament with its movement from plea to praise is an act of boldness. Underneath the pain and anguish, the anger and despair, lies a confidence that allows and even compels the psalmist to give voice to the darkness. Out of the depths comes the cries of the psalmist, and the cries of all those who have followed. The psalms of lament speak the unspeakable and name the unnamable. In doing so, they offer the hope for transformation. This is not a cheap hope that can be easily confused with optimism. Rather it is a hope wrought in relationship and trust. The depth of pain expressed in the laments is all too real. Yet so too is the possibility that this pain can be transformed—will be transformed—into praise.

In the Psalms, the God who is faithful, powerful, and generous not only hears the cries but also responds. To be sure, something remarkable does indeed happen in the lament. God surely behaves in ways that are liberating, redeeming, and life-giving. Through the lament, the psalmist invites each of us deeper into the life of faith. A warning must be given though: This descent leads into disorientation, into the depths of human experience. It is only through this descent that new life and a new orientation may be discovered.

Orientation—Disorientation—New Orientation

This section will focus on Brueggemann's scheme of orientation—disorientation—new orientation with particular attention paid to the process of disorientation.[13] Building upon the seminal work of

12. Brueggemann, "Psalms as Prayer," 33.

13. Brueggemann, *Message of the Psalms*; Brueggemann, *Praying the Psalms*; Brueggemann, "Psalms and the Life of Faith," 3–32; and Brueggemann, *Spirituality of the Psalms*.

Westermann, Brueggemann's scheme further develops the internal movement from plea to praise within the laments. It is important to note that, for Brueggemann, this scheme is not to be seen as a rigid, unbending form into which every psalm has to be forced. It is not a narrow, uncompromising rule. Said another way, the scheme is not a way to jam round pegs into square holes. Rather, the scheme serves as a way of understanding, a way of conceptualizing. It is, at its best, a "principle of organization."[14]

This scheme provides a way of seeing the whole of the Psalms as foundational to the life of faith. That is, the laments in all of the despairing complaints, the outraged accusations, the broken petitions, the persistent appeals, and the desire for vengeance are not outside the life of faith. On the contrary, all of life, all of human experience, is embraced within the covenantal relationship with God. The movement from orientation to disorientation to new orientation shows in clear and profound ways "that what goes on in the Psalms is peculiarly in touch with what goes on in our life."[15] On first glance, the lament in all of its anguish may seem to be in opposition to faith, at least a faith that sees only light, goodness, and contentment. It is, instead, a way to move deeper into a faith which is transformative, a faith where God does indeed make a difference. The Psalms, as clearly seen in Brueggemann's scheme, stand as a counter-narrative to the lemming-like rush toward a faith which is really only stoicism and resignation disguised. As John Endres says, "The Psalms tutor us in the language of prayer; they teach us new ways of praying and more expressive ways of articulating our hopes and fear, our joys and sorrows."[16]

For Brueggemann, the life of faith is centered on two decisive moves which are always occurring.[17] The first is a movement out of what he calls a settled orientation and into a season of disorientation. This movement may happen because some circumstance has changed. It may be the onset of an illness, the loss of a job, the

---

14. Brueggemann, *Spirituality of the Psalms*, viii.
15. Brueggemann, *Spirituality of the Psalms*, ix–x.
16. Endres, "Psalms and Spirituality," 154.
17. Brueggemann, *Message of the Psalms*.

death of a loved one, the recognition of sin and the pain caused by that recognition. It could even be something as simple as a growing awareness that life is not always fair and that bad things happen for no apparent reason. No matter. This movement from the security of the known into the chaos of the unknown evokes feelings of rage, resentment, anguish, and sadness. This movement captures Westermann's idea of the plea in the lament.

The second movement is from this chaotic disorientation into a new orientation. It is a movement characterized by the assurance that God has heard and responded to the cries of the psalmist. Action has been taken. God has indeed intervened as God is supposed to do. From Sheol, from the pit, new life emerges and the response in reply to this new life is one of thanksgiving and praise.

These two movements might be visualized like this:[18]

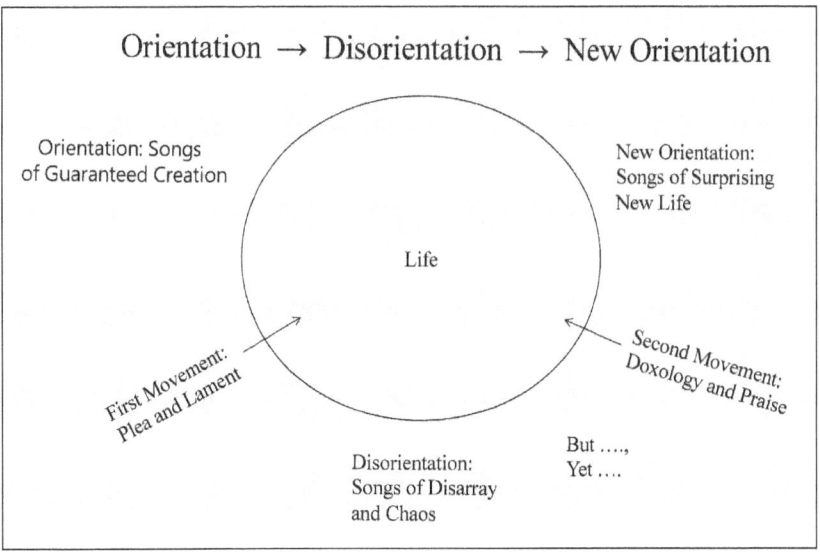

From the settled stance of orientation where life is good and contentment is the order of the day, the lament psalms recognize there is more with which to contend. Bad things happen. Circumstances change. Loss occurs. Grief and sorrow break the heart. The deep of the pit is keenly felt. Life is turned upside down and inside out.

18. Brueggemann, *Spirituality of the Psalms*.

Chaos reigns. Lament, deep and loud and persistent, is now called for. This is the first movement. The cry of lament speaks the terrible truth of disorientation.

However, this terrible truth does not have the last word. Something happens as the lament is prayed aloud. The pleas and the petitions all reach God and God responds. Disorientation moves toward a new orientation, towards a new life. The Psalms are never clear about exactly how this movement happens. It is usually marked by the word, "but." Yes, bad things have happened. Yes, the anguish is real. Yes, Sheol is a dark place. The truth of life must indeed be spoken and named. While it may feel like the disorientation will last forever and from which there is no escape, there is another narrative waiting. This narrative begins with the great and majestic word, "But." This word tells us the story is not over. There is more to come.

What comes is God. God responds and acts. Disorientation does not last forever. Through God's mighty acts, a new orientation unfolds. New life emerges. Of course, the lament is not forgotten, but somehow there is a transformative experience that overshadows the acute pain of the lament. The movement is then into doxology and praise to God for being rescued and delivered and saved and healed. This movement into a new orientation is characterized by a "rush of positive responses, including delight, amazement, wonder, awe, gratitude, and thanksgiving."[19]

Orientation

The psalms of orientation are just that—psalms that give voice to a settled, sure faith. These psalms reflect the assurance of God's watchful care over God's creation and God's people. They reflect the assurance that God is indeed trustworthy and reliable. These psalms are the poetry that express gratitude and confidence in God that comes from the long ago past and has been known from generation to generation. Brueggemann writes, "Life, as reflected

---

19. Brueggemann, *Spirituality of the Psalms*, 11.

The Psalms of Lament and the Transformation of Sorrow

in the psalms, is not troubled or threatened, but is seen as the well-ordered world intended by God."[20]

The sense of orientation found in the psalms expresses the belief that the world is reliable because God has deemed it so. God's handiwork of creation is trustworthy and known. God is in control and watches over all. Thus, orientation means that our human life is ordered and possesses a sense of well-being that is deserved and expected. Orientation means the great blessings of life are recognized in prayer and worship. However, the reality of life and our common human experience is that life is not always well-ordered and secure. There is another side to the equation that cries out for recognition. This is the reality of disorientation.

Disorientation

As Brueggemann suggests, in addition to the times of blessing, "Human life consists in anguished seasons of hurt, alienation, suffering and death. These evoke rage, resentment, self-pity, and hatred."[21] The security and solid footing of the orientation disappears in times of loss and change. Nothing is certain. All the old ways, the old understandings, collapse under the weight of darkness. Brueggemann's idea of disorientation parallels Westermann's articulation of the structure of the lament plea.

In times of disorientation, questions are asked that have no answers. How long will God forget? How long will God be hidden? How long must pain be born? How long will the enemy be exalted? There are no answers to these terrible questions. They echo off the empty sky. To live into these questions is to face the deep darkness. There is no way to avoid it. The psalmist gives voice to this anguished part of our human experience. And there are times when the words and questions catch in the throat, when the utterance cannot be finished, when the darkness is so oppressive and painful that all is left is a groan. The unanswered questions cut

---

20. Brueggemann, *Spirituality of the Psalms*, 20.
21. Brueggemann, *Message of the Psalms*, 8.

to the quick. How long, O Lord? How long? There is no certainty on to which to hold. The disorientation fully recognizes just how dangerous life really is. The settled and comfortable knowing of the times of orientation has faded away into the unsettled and uncomfortable unknowing of the times of disorientation. Both times are real. Both times are true. The disorientation points to the fact that something is acutely amiss in the relationship. Something has occurred that needs to be made aright.

The psalms of disorientation continue to say that even though something has happened and the orientation has turned into disorientation, everything must be voiced. It all must be brought to speech. It must be said aloud. There is no value in silence, isolation, and denial. And if everything—and every feeling—must be voiced, then it must also be addressed to God, who is, as Brueggemann says, "the final reference for all of life."[22]

The recognition of the disorientation gives permission to speak all that it unspeakable and name all that is unnamable. Nothing is to be held back. No matter what the feeling or experience, the psalms are clear in their urgency to speak and name. In these psalms, there are cries for deliverance, for healing, for life, for mercy, for forgiveness, for help, for vengeance, for relief, for hope, for attention, for presence, for strength.

The times of disorientation call for desperate measures and for urgent action. It is not a time for "making nice." Too much is at stake. God is expected, even in the disorientation, to hear the fullness of the cries because that is who God has proven to be. God is expected to hear. God is expected to act. God is expected to deliver. However, God's hearing, acting, and delivering are not always easy things to bear. The psalms of disorientation tell us that the darkness is indeed real. Brueggemann puts it like this:

> These psalms are dangerous. They lead into places of deep darkness, where denial and deception try to rule the day. They lead us to the place where we have to say this is how it really is, to a place where not everything can be reduced to polite and civil musings and gestures. They

---

22. Brueggemann, *Spirituality of the Psalms*, 27.

The Psalms of Lament and the Transformation of Sorrow

lead us, ever boldly, to think unthinkable thoughts and utter unutterable words. But our honest experience, both personal and public, attests to the resilience of the darkness, in spite of us. The remarkable thing about Israel is that it did not banish or deny the darkness from its religious enterprise. It embraces the darkness as the very stuff of new life.[23]

How, indeed, does the psalmist get to "the very stuff of new life?" Something happens in the psalms. But exactly what? Between the voicing of the plea and into the singing of the praise, there is some sort of transformation which takes place. Never in the psalms are we told what this transformation entails. A mystery occurs in the movement between plea to praise, from disorientation towards new orientation. There is no clear and certain answer as to what makes this movement possible. Nevertheless, it is a most remarkable transformation.

The psalms of lament continually attest to the undeniable fact that something has changed: "Life is transformed; health is restored; enemies are resisted and destroyed; death is averted; shalom is given again. The structure of the poem expresses this change."[24] The function of the great and mighty word, "But," points to this transformative dimension. Whatever happened, it surely had a profound impact on the psalmist, for there is a new and renewed sense of trust and gratitude.

The "But" in the times of disorientation reflects the mysterious movement from hopelessness to hope, from darkness to light. To be sure, this movement is never easy or even natural. It comes with a great cost. To be transformed in the crucible of lament is to know intimately the pain and joy of life. The hope for transformation is grounded in the covenantal relationship with the God who is steadfast, abounds in mercy, and forgives daily. Said another way, the radical word of this transformation, "But" is a way of speaking of the good news. God always has the last word. Death is overcome.

---

23. Brueggemann, *Message of the Psalms*, 53.
24. Brueggemann, "From Hurt to Joy," 73.

New Orientation

The new orientation characterizes the second movement away from disorientation. Most often, the Psalms bear witness to "the very stuff of new life," as Brueggemann put it.[25] This new life is the great surprise of the Psalms. New life comes as a gift when it seemed it might be lost forever. It is important to note here that this new life is not the old life. The new orientation is not a recapitulation of the old orientation. It is not a means of going back to the "good ol' days." It is what it says it is: new.

Moreover, the psalmist knows there can no longer be business as usual. Just as the Psalms acknowledge the existence of the times of settled comfortableness and times of distress and trouble, they also recognize that our human life is also marked by times of wonderful surprise when we are simply overwhelmed by the gracious gifts of God offered to us, freely.

The times of distress and trouble, voiced raw and eloquently, give way to times of newness and renewal. As Sheppard writes, "The psalms also seek to establish the fact that, no matter how often suppliants threaten to doubt it in the course of their anguished complaints, God can answer their questions and has power to change things for them."[26] The "But" points toward the newness, toward the possibility of transformation. It points, indeed, toward miracle. The life of faith, grounded in relationship, has been once more reaffirmed.

The movement from orientation to disorientation to new orientation is the movement of God across the face of the void. There is nothing natural about this movement. Rather, it reflects the power and faithfulness of God who makes all things new, who gives new life, who brings us out of Sheol, who makes all things possible.

Brueggemann's scheme provides a rich container in which to hold the Psalms. In the life of faith, the lament remains difficult as it should. There is nothing easy about lament. But prayed in its

---

25. Brueggemann, *Message of the Psalms*, 53.
26. Shepperd, "Theology and the Book of Psalms," 144–145.

fullness and voiced from the depths, it provides a bold and subversive act of faith. From out of the depths, the lament teaches us, and has taught us, that the darkness will not overcome us. Our pain can be spoken and named. Our hurt can be lifted up and heard. Our cries can come from our heart. We can rest assured nothing, nothing at all, can separate us from the love of God. We can be transformed even once more.

Implications for Pastoral Care and Clinical Pastoral Education

The call comes into the Pastoral Care office late one afternoon. The nurse says, "Chaplain, would you please come see Mr. Smith in 5080? He has just gotten some bad news and . . ." Her voice trails off. The rest of this nurse's referral is left unsaid. It turns out Mr. Smith, a 45-year-old married man with two teenage daughters, has learned he has pancreatic cancer. The doctors say he has about three or four months to live, six at the most. Upon arrival on the unit, the nurse tells the chaplain that Mr. Smith is "upset." She suggests that a pastoral visit from the chaplain would make him "feel better." In other words, if Mr. Smith "feels better," then he will be an easier patient for which to care. How the chaplain responds to this referral depends, in part, on his or her theological understanding of the psalms of lament and the process of orientation— disorientation—new orientation.

Implications for Pastoral Care

In pastoral care, the Psalms can be used as a resource to provide comfort to those who are hurting. The psalms of lament speak to the many needs of the sick, the dying, the discouraged, and the enraged. The psalms of lament indeed speak the unspeakable and name the unnamable. In that sense, they provide assurance that the person is not alone in his or her feelings. Others across the centuries of faith have dealt with circumstances which have evoked similar feelings. Donald Capps says the psalms of lament can be used as pastoral resources for two reasons: (1) Because the psalms of lament speak of universal feelings and experiences, people are able to identify with the psalmist and see that the psalmist expresses their feelings more profoundly than they could themselves. The ancient words still ring true today. The ancient words still possess power. (2) Since the psalms of lament are mostly non-specific about the circumstances which are bringing about distress and trouble, people can use the words to fit their own situation. The enemies in the psalms can be any thing or any one.[27]

The psalms of lament can be used to address such pastoral care situations as terminal illness and death (e.g., Psalms 6, 23, 41, 139), bereavement (e.g., Psalm 90), old age (e.g., Psalm 71), grief over past mistakes (e.g., Psalm 38), and, of course, there are other situations that could be named as well. The point here is to acknowledge that the Psalms offer a way embrace the fullness of human life including all the experiences of hurt, sorrow, and pain.

Much of the pastoral care task, at least in the hospital setting, involves the dynamic of grief. Grief is ever-present, always close at hand. Mr. Smith knows grief intimately now. His whole life has been turned upside down. I often tell the nursing staff and my CPE students that my job is not to necessarily make someone feel better. In fact, my job may be to help some feel much worse. Mr. Smith may need to feel a whole lot worse before he can even begin to feel different, much less better.

For some pastors and seminary students, pastoral care means giving someone an answer. It means offering a Scripture verse or two, maybe a prayer, designed to speak words of comfort and hope, which, regretfully, only serve to deny and avoid the situation of disorientation. My pastoral care with Mr. Smith would not be to try to make him "feel better." He has every right to feel bad, to be angry, to be sad, to be depressed. He is now living in the valley of the shadow. He is descending into the pit. Now is not the time to patronize him with a pat on the head and a cliché.

---

27. Capps, "Psalms," 969–70.

What Mr. Smith needs in this time of trial, I believe, is a lament. He needs to be able to cry out to God, to complain about the unfairness of this diagnosis and the fact he will not see his teenagers graduate from college. He needs to make his appeal to God. There is, of course, no guarantee that God will take away the cancer. The pastoral objective here is to give Mr. Smith the time and space to move deep into disorientation. The pastoral purpose is to allow Mr. Smith, even to give him permission, to grieve and grieve fully what this loss means for him and his family. Mr. Smith needs someone to stand with him in the space of disorientation.

Pastoral care is not about "fixing" the pain. The temptation to "fix" a person's pain or try to take it away in pastoral relationships is the great seduction of ministry. The role of the pastor is not so much as to "fix" as it is to be present. Often I hear a patient like Mr. Smith say something like, "Chaplain, I need to tell you something that I can't tell my pastor. I know he (or she) won't hear it." Comments like this tell me about the great anxiety pastors and seminary students may have when faced with a situation of grief and sorrow and there is nothing that can be done to take away the pain. The anxiety driven by feelings of helplessness propels the pastor to find ways to deny and avoid the lament. In conscious and unconscious ways, the pastor may give the message to his or her parishioner that the feelings of lament are unacceptable in the life of faith. Lament is then seen as an act of unbelief rather than a bold act of faith. Such a message does nothing to relieve the feelings of lament. On the contrary, it only serves to drive the feelings underground in shame and embarrassment.

A theology that has no place for lament is left only with thin, inadequate murmurings. The covenantal relationship is reduced to a mere shell, maneuvered about with smoke and mirrors rather than serious and faithful engagement. As Brueggemann says, "Covenant minus lament is finally a practice of denial, cover-up, and pretense..."[28] A theology which takes our covenantal relationship with God seriously must then also take the laments seriously. One cannot happen without the other.

---

28. Brueggemann, "Costly Loss of Lament," 102.

The laments ground the practice of pastoral care in the reality of the human experience. The practice of pastoral care which acknowledges the lament and its accompanying disorientation is then positioned to also acknowledge the prayers of thanksgiving and praise which come with the new orientation. Somehow, as Mr. Smith laments, he moves into, however gingerly, doxology as he gives thanks for his life.

Implications for Clinical Pastoral Education

The setting of CPE within the hospital invites disorientation. There is more disorientation in the hospital than elsewhere. Patients wait anxiously for tests to come back, surrender their lives and autonomy to a surgeon, subject their bodies to chemotherapy and radiation, and submit their dignity to the indignities of a hospital gown. The hospital reeks of disorientation. Into this setting, seminary students enter CPE programs and all the disorientation which awaits them.

In my experience as a CPE supervisor, I have found that, more and more, young seminary students enter into this process with a rigid and unbending theological stance that is characterized by certainty and smug assurance. There seems to be a secure and unyielding orientation set by tradition. However, there is no place for reflection, for questions, for musings, for poetry. Correct doctrine trumps all wonder. Not surprisingly, then, there is quite a clash when these students encounter disorientation with patients, family members, and staff. Answers found in textbooks fall flat in the ICU when anguished questions about removing life support from a sixty-five-year-old woman are raised. There is no certainty when sitting the ED with the parents of a seventeen-year-old boy who has coded and died on Easter morning. Tradition does not help when a long hoped-for infant is born with unexpected multiple anomalies and grief pours out of the parents.

The challenge in CPE, it seems to me, is to facilitate an experience which honors the initial orientation of the students, invites them into disorientation and, at the same time, points towards a new orientation. Not all seminary students are able to succeed in the CPE process. The movement into disorientation shapes the profound learning that occurs. The seminary students who are able to risk their treasured beliefs are able to open themselves up to the possibility of transformation.

In other words, the disorientation students experience with patients and family members soon turns toward their own disorientation. Their world and how they understood it theologically is turned upside down and inside out. Old set formulas of prayer and Scripture verses offer no help, and in fact, may be rejected. Something else is required. The CPE process invites the students into their own disorientation with their feelings of hurt and pain. The more a student has experienced the transforming power of the lament in his or her own life, the more he or she will be able to be present with other persons in their laments.

Learning about one's own laments is not for the faint of heart. It requires a movement down into the depths. It calls for a bold act of faith which is new and maybe even radical. Such learning runs counter to our cultural expectation that we somehow "move on" when faced with pain and sorrow. Such learning requires the subversive acts of active listening, attending to the pain, and giving voice to the voiceless. "The theological significance of the personal lament," writes Westermann, "lies first of all in the fact that it gives voice to suffering. The lament is the language of suffering; in it suffering is given the dignity of language."[29]

It is this language, this language of suffering, this language of poetry, that CPE can teach seminary students. The challenge—and the risk—of CPE is not to deny the laments and their place in learning the discipline of pastoral care. The challenge and risk is to be able to name the danger in such transformative learning.

Mr. Smith needs—and deserves—at least that much.

---

29. Westermann, "Role of the Lament," 31.

Conclusion

The psalms of lament reflect the real engagement of every real dimension of life in covenantal relationship with God. Nothing is held back. As such, the psalms of lament make a radical and bold statement of faith: that even in the awful times of anguish and sorrow, God still attends to all of life, all of creation, all of God's people. No one is left out or left behind. The laments tell us that nothing, nothing at all, is out of bounds. Nothing is outside of God's gaze.

As poetry, the psalms of lament reflect the danger and mystery of transformation. Somehow and someway, even the worst of circumstances cannot last forever. The psalmist teaches us that as our hearts are poured out, God does indeed hear our cries and respond. The danger and mystery is that the situation is changed. We are not told how. We just know that the change has happened. We are witness to it. The danger and mystery is that, in addition to the situation being changed, we too are changed. I am changed. I am a witness to God's steadfastness in my life. The psalms of lament, in all their pain and sorrow and in all their praise and thanksgiving, contain the mystery of transformation. They contain the hope for transformation.

2

Silent Night

It is around noon on Christmas Eve. My beeper calls out the number for the Pediatric Intensive Care Unit. The nurse tells me an eight-year-old boy named John is being flown by helicopter to the hospital. He is in a coma, and his dad is flying with him. "Not on Christmas Eve," I say to myself, "*not* on Christmas Eve."

I meet John's dad in the Pediatric Intensive Care waiting room. No one else is there. The hospital is quiet. It is Christmas Eve. He tells me John's mom is on the way in the car. He is very tearful as he waits to see his son. "I can't believe this is happening. I can't believe this is happening," he says over and over. The shock and disbelief are numbing.

I ask him to tell me what happened. As we sit, he tells me the story of the past few days many times. He starts in a different place each time, but he always ends with the same question—"Why?" He wonders how all the symptoms could have been missed, how he and John's mom just thought John was tired and needed more rest, how they had no idea he was this sick, and then, how he was finally rushed here to the hospital. As he tells this, he breaks down and begins to cry. He beats his hands on the arms of the chair. I listen to him. I feel helpless.

He cries for a long time. We sit in the silence of his tears. There are no words now. Quietly, he says he feels like he should have been able to do something different. He says he should have known that something was wrong with John. "Daddies are supposed to know," he screams. "Daddies are supposed to know." His guilt and helplessness are overwhelming. I think, "Dear God, please not on Christmas Eve."

John's mom arrives. Around 3:00 p.m. the doctors tell them John is brain-dead. There is nothing more that can be done for him. Once more, we sit in silence as they hold each other while their tears flow and their hearts break.

So the vigil begins. We gather in the Pediatric Intensive Care Unit. It is a large room. A small Christmas tree stands in the corner. A radio plays carols in the background. There are Christmas decorations on the walls. John is the only patient in the unit. As the sun sets and darkness settles over the land, the lights around John's bed are the only ones that are on. We pull up some chairs around his bed. Then, one by one, the doctors and the nurses bring over their chairs and sit with us. No one speaks. It seems each person is lost in thought, maybe pondering in their hearts the mystery of life and death that is to be a part of this Christmas Eve. There is a sense of community as we wait.

Softly, John's mom and dad begin to tell stories about him. They tell of his fights with his brothers, how he always liked school, how he loved soccer, and about his first girlfriend. They tell stories that are funny and sad, stories of his triumphs and tragedies, stories that are filled with such special love and affection as they share their son with us. Then, slowly, we all begin to tell some of our own stories of school, of growing up, families, girlfriends and boyfriends. It is the right thing to do. Somehow, there is laughter and grace woven in all the tears and hurt.

As John's mom and dad talk, they stroke his hair and caress his cheeks. In a whisper, John's dad begins to talk about Christmas. He voice drops. His tears fall. He tells of unopened presents under the tree, of special gifts and surprises. Haltingly, he tells of his

Silent Night

hopes and dreams he had for John, and that he tried to be a good daddy.

Finally, it is time to turn off the life-support machines. The vigil is over. It is finished. He mom cries very hard, and then, gently, tenderly, softly, she bends down to her son. She kisses him on the forehead, and says, "I love you."

> *Silent night, holy night,*
> *All is calm, all is bright*
> *Round yon Virgin Mother and child.*
> *Holy infant so tender and mild,*
> *Sleep in heavenly peace,*
> *Sleep in heavenly peace.*

With John's dad holding his hand, I say a prayer for him. My tears blind me. My heart chokes me. There are some words said about, "for unto us a child is born, unto us a son is given."

With his dad holding his hand, John's heart is stilled. There is peace on earth.

As I have remembered that night, somehow and someway, the time was holy. In the darkness, among the stories and the carols, the angels of heaven cried. On that cold night, we had no gifts to give. There was no gold or frankincense or myrrh, only the precious gift of each other. As we told our stories, we gave of our very selves, each to the other—maybe in unspeakable and sacred ways—but give we did.

In those long hours that were too short, in the laughter that was filled with tears, in the hope that was filled with fear, Christ was born and John died. A son is given.

Sleep in heavenly peace, little John, sleep in heavenly peace.

3

The Clinical Rhombus Revisited
Learning Through Resistance and Change

IN *THE TEACHING AND Learning of Psychotherapy*, Ekstein and Wallerstein form a clinical rhombus which depicts the complex psychological and social nature of the learning environment.[1] The rhombus includes the administrator (A), supervisor (S), student therapist (T), and patient (P), and each component serves a different function. In the rhombus, different corners and triangles are continually being activated. It is in this context that learning takes place.

In writing of the rhombus, Ekstein and Wallerstein observe that

> as the student in his corner faces the other three corners of his clinical world, he confronts three kind of problems which, we hope to demonstrate, are but external representations of typical inner situations. He is to help the patient and has to acquire skills in order to cope with the seeming chaos that the illness of the patient, for the most part, represents to him. To the supervisor he brings his own chaos, his own difficulties and lack of knowledge and skill, in order to receive help toward the furtherance of his own process of increasing mastery and growing

1. Ekstein and Wallerstein, *Teaching and Learning*, 3–15.

The Clinical Rhombus Revisited

competence. And finally, the administrator represents chiefly the conditions and requirements of the clinical situation that the student has to meet, and with the approval or disapproval of the work he is doing. As he goes on with the task of acquiring psychotherapeutic skills, he has to face these same aspects of himself. He has to cope with the archaic, unorganized aspects of his professional self, he has to develop skills, areas of technical and human competence, and he has to struggle with the task of having to live by regulations and of having to live up to professional ideas.[2]

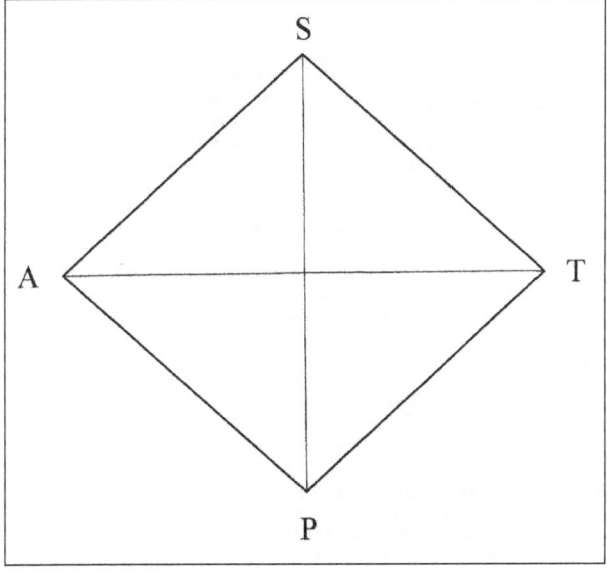

Clinical Pastoral Education has used the clinical rhombus as a model for reflecting on the art of supervision and the effects of different arenas of learning upon pastoral formation and education. For our purposes, we designate the student therapist (T) corner of the rhombus as CPE *resident* (R). The patient (P) corner, as we will show, can be changed from an individual person or patient to a community or system orientation where P comes to represent

2. Ekstein and Wallerstein, *Teaching and Learning,* 3.

the CPE resident's whole clinical assignment in ministry, or *parish*. The *supervisor* (S) and the *administrator* (A) designations remain unchanged, although the actual persons representing the S corner and A corner may change.

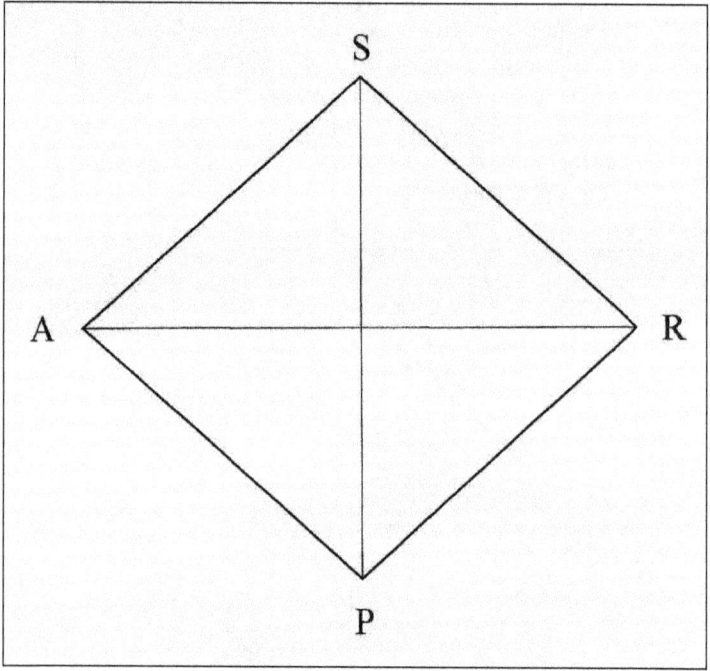

In previous years, when training basic and advanced CPE students in our center, we have intentionally and unintentionally utilized the clinical rhombus in our curriculum. In the 1991–1992 residency program, we chose to apply the clinical rhombus rather intentionally to the clinical training process. The impact of this curriculum focus is significant in looking at pastoral formation as well as assessing resistance and conflict in students, supervisors, and administrators due to changes in the clinical rhombus.[3]

In previous groups of first- and second-year residents, we had changed the supervisor (S) corner in the clinical rhombus. In one unit, one of us (Carole, for instance) would supervise two or

3. Mueller and Kell, *Coping with Conflict*, 3–38; and Friedman, *Generation to Generation*, 17–19.

The Clinical Rhombus Revisited

three residents, and in the next unit, the other supervisor (Logan) might supervise these same residents. The change was primarily in individual supervision, and we continued to co-supervise in the group process. As we have co-supervised together over the past four years, it has become increasingly clear to us that the most significant learning in CPE occurs within the peer group process. Consequently, in our center much more time is spent in group process than in individual supervision. For example, we have four ninety-minute group seminars a week versus only one hour of individual supervision.

We changed the supervisory aspect of the rhombus based on our assessment of the students' learning needs as well as input from the students on supervisor preference. This change in the supervisory focus in the rhombus did serve to heighten anxiety creatively. However, because the change focused on the individual resident (R) and supervisor (S), personal issues were heightened with little impact on pastoral authority and identity with patients or peer group.

Learning does indeed take place as the supervisor (S) corner of the clinical rhombus is changed. Students are anxious as supervisory assignments are changed and they are faced with establishing new relationships. However, we did not want to continually focus solely on the supervisor-resident relationship. Instead, we wanted to intentionally apply systems thinking and theory to the dynamics around the clinical rhombus. As we will show, learning can take place through resistance and change as the clinical rhombus is intentionally used and reflected upon.

Any change produces anxiety. Systems thinking and theory says that, in response to change, the message given is one that says, "don't change," or more powerfully, "change back." This is the principle of homeostasis.[4] However, change is inherent in ministry, in relationships, and in systems. Reflection upon change and its effects—resistance, blame, defensiveness—in the use of the clinical rhombus provides a rich arena for learning the art of pastoral care.

---

4. Friedman, *Generation to Generation*, 23–25.

The Care of Souls

Case Study

The change in the clinical rhombus that was implemented in the 1991–1992 residency program was a change in how we, as supervisors, understood and conceptualized the patient corner (P) of the rhombus. We moved from focusing on the individual patient to focusing on the whole clinical area or parish. Our residency year began in September. In January, when we were a few weeks into the second unit, clinical assignments were reviewed, discussed, and changed. Rather than simply changing the supervisor corner (S), we changed the parish corner (P) for the residents. This change was initiated by us as a dialogical process, and we sought input from the residents about how they saw their own learning process and pastoral functioning. However, the final assignments were determined by us.

It is important to note this change in the parish corner (P) of the clinical rhombus was brought about by several different factors. One factor was a more intentional utilization of visitation statistics. The residents record each pastoral visit they make along with the unit and the referral source, if any. These reports are submitted weekly. As early as the fall unit evaluations, each resident was asked to review their statistics for the twelve-week period. The pastoral care secretary compiled a summary report for each resident. The residents' ability to assess and apply the hard data of the statistics to pastoral formation issues was limited and defensive in the fall evaluations.

A second factor was a new management focus of the hospital administration. The administration had been in an educational process of reviewing and critiquing management styles and directions for leadership as early as a winter management retreat at the beginning of 1991. This management focus was called "Total Quality Management." The models used were presented to hospital management staff by an ex-Lutheran pastor who had completed a CPE residency. He was currently in charge of quality management in a regional medical center in Indiana. This, combined with a

The Clinical Rhombus Revisited

Xerox Corporation presentation on quality management, reflected the concept of *paradigm*, which, as Stephen Covey notes,

> comes from the Greek. It was originally a scientific term, and is more commonly used today to mean a model, theory, perception, assumption, or frame of reference. In the more general sense, it's the way we "see" the world—not in terms of visual sight, but in terms of perceiving, understanding, interpreting . . . Paradigms are inseparable from character. "Being" is "seeing" in the human dimension. And what we "see" is highly interrelated to what we "are." We can't go very far to change our seeing without simultaneously changing our being and vice versa.[5]

This concept of paradigm raised the prospect that the inability of the chaplain residents to utilize hard data might be related to their pastoral paradigms. Our question then became, "How can we help them *see* who they *are* in ministry?"

A third factor was our assessment of the parish assignments in our center as well as the residents' own learning processes and future plans. Methodist Medical Center (MMC) in Dallas is a 463-bed, general/acute trauma center. A sister hospital in our system is Southeastern Methodist Hospital (SMH), a 108-bed rural community hospital. What did ER ministry at MMC offer a resident who was going to be a local church pastor? What did solo ministry at SMH offer a resident who was planning a career as a hospital chaplain? What did ministry to a renal transplant unit and general surgery unit facilitate in a two-year veteran of less-than-successful rural pastorates?

These three factors prompted us to change our focus in the clinical rhombus to have the patient corner represent the whole clinical parish. This change created an opportunity for assessing and utilizing our center's resources more intentionally for pastoral education, making it possible to look at who we are in ministry. Paradigms were challenged.

The shift in pastoral assignments and paradigms began as a dialogical process. The residents were encouraged to reflect upon

---

5. Covey, *Seven Habits*, 23, 32.

their pastoral visitation as highlighted by their statistics, their future goals for ministry, and their own present learning goals and/or learning insights. The group's response to this reflection was defensive and resistant. When challenged on this stance, the residents as a group stated no specific insights or pastoral concerns, save the desire to maintain the original assignments. Change was to be avoided at all costs. The resistance to change in the outer world of the clinical rhombus paralleled the resistance to change in the inner world of the resident.

At this point, we nevertheless implemented the pastoral changes we saw appropriate. These changes moved the Methodist Medical Center (MMC) resident for the ICU and general surgery floors to Southeastern Methodist Hospital (SMH). The resident who covered SMH was moved to MMC to cover the ICU, SCN, and other general floors. The resident in the renal transplant and rehabilitation units was maintained there but moved out of the SCN. Finally, the second unit Basic resident was kept in his current parish assignment, but his responsibility to the ER was increased.

These changes allowed the resident who planned to take a local church position the opportunity to move out of the high-paced intensity of the ICU ministry at MMC and move into the more consistent, low-stress, general illness atmosphere of SMH. It challenged the resident who had left his last parish feeling less than successful to work at succeeding in ministry on his renal/transplant unit with patients and staff. It enabled the resident who planned to enter hospital ministry at the end of his second-year residency to work through his personal problems in a more structured setting at MMC rather than at the isolated rural setting of SMH. Finally, it increased the basic resident's responsibility and anxiety toward more self-directed learning in the ER.

As could be expected given the initial defensiveness and lack of reflection, each resident's reaction to these changes was intense and resistant. The primary behavior was blame-centered. Each resident stated there must be *one resident* (and obviously not them) who was doing so poorly that his or her assignments had to be changed— "It must be his fault because he is having

The Clinical Rhombus Revisited

personal problems," or "It must be her fault because she wants to be in a local church." We, as supervisors, were blamed for making arbitrary changes in the assignments with no rhyme or reason. A scapegoat—or identified patient—needed to be found.[6] When the residents reached an impasse, we intervened by questioning the significance of blame in the learning process. We reiterated that the original negotiation was not about finding fault, but rather about opportunity; not about inability, but about future goals and effectiveness; not about maintaining the status quo, but about opportunity for excellence in ministry and pastoral formation. The residents gradually began to assess their own projections. The tenuous trek into self-reflection on pastoral formation was begun.

Several assumptions surfaced as the changes were instituted. Although we had stressed that the staff and patients would need pastoral support from the departing and entering residents, the first operating assumption was that "the resident is the only one affected." This was demonstrated as the residents' timing for the announced changes gave staff no time for adequate processing. A second assumption was the need for self-protection. Risk taking, confrontation, and challenge had been blocked in the group process at an implicit nonverbal level. While the residents saw themselves as open to reflection and self-evaluation, the opportunity for change evoked fear. Third, pastoral authority was directly impacted as the group initially acted as a collegial team. Authority issues surfaced in resistance, hostility, and blame. These evidenced a hierarchy of pastoral assignments: the ICU is good, general medicine is bad; MMC is good, SMH is bad; high-crisis acute floors are more prestigious than general maternity and well-baby floors. The fourth assumption was that learning occurs only in highly controlled and contained environments. A sentiment like "change is disruptive to learning" was voiced by each resident at some point. A theological dilemma evoked a fifth assumption. In a Sunday morning worship service, a resident preached the gospel message that, even though Jesus was and is the Savior, the disciples expected a much different outcome than the cross. The message

---

6. Friedman, *Generation to Generation*, 19–23.

created a powerful confrontation with the injunction to "practice what you preach." This resident and the group saw her and their resistance to the new assignments as paralleling the disciples' lack of faith as Jesus pursued the paradoxical path of salvation through crucifixion and resurrection.

The reflective pastor is challenged to move away from *technical rationality* as the key to successful professional practice.[7] The professional competency required for pastoral ministry (whether it be in the local church, hospital, or institution) requires an *artistry* that is not taught by *cognitive* means. While hopefully this is apparent to all of us in Clinical Pastoral Education, the challenge of *how to educate this competency* is real. The process we are describing was implemented to move beyond technical rationality and stimulate in-depth reaction and reflection on our ability to "give up freedom . . . in order to gain the freedom that comes with new levels of understanding and control. Freedom is discipline—the step beyond progressive education . . . freedom to perceive, compare and coordinate many different meanings and sets the stage for an eventual commitment based on richer understanding."[8]

Pastoral Learning Results

After the changes we have described, the residents completed self-evaluations of this winter unit. We quote from their self-evaluations in order to illustrate the learning which occurred. One resident wrote:

> I felt like I was dragging in December. Ministry was not a joy, in fact it was usually quite a drag . . . learning to take more initiative and exert more authority in the way that I think about and do visits. . . . 4T increased with more than 100 visits, 8 Rehab tripled and 8T increased about threefold, with corresponding increases in family visits . . . taking ownership of my ministry and trying to

---

7. Schön, *Educating the Reflective Practitioner*, 3–43.
8. Schön, *Educating the Reflective Practitioner*, 123.

"create" ministry, I have also been able to "hang out" and be seen with staff.

Another resident stated:

> In theory, I was in favor of the changers in clinical assignments. But in my heart, I didn't want to do it at first. The biggest reason was related to "talking and sharing." In making the switch, I knew I would be leaving people who knew of my current situation and that I would be going to be a place where no one knew of my struggles. That challenged me in many of my pastoral relationships. One way it helped me was making me realize that putting some distance between my own struggles and my ministry helped me put more energy into my ministry. For example, previous to making the switch, I would rarely if ever fill up my patient visitation sheet for one day. But the first day back to the medical center, I filled up a full page and part of another.

Still another resident observed:

> Ministry was easy in the ICU. There was always so much and such obvious stuff to do I never had to think—just move from patient and family to the next. . . Though I still have an ICU, and continue to visit every patient/family there daily, I get to the other floors with much more regularity. Life in general is a little slower but there is more than enough to do. I think my strongest ministry is no longer in ICU. I would say that my greatest amount of time in ministry now is with staff. I cannot believe the number of persons who walk in my door or grab me on the floor and want to talk. Work stress, personal problems, seem to abound among them. On the floors I am finding a great deal of satisfaction and challenge in working with the same patients that I "overlooked" so easily in the medical center. Older, chronic heart, pulmonary, and stroke victims are the mainstay. I have learned that these patients come and go with regularity and that the staff are very attached to them.

Finally, a fourth resident noted:

> Last unit, more often than not, I would wait until the ER staff called before going there. This unit I've tried to go through the ER several times a day . . . I've been able to establish relationships with patients early on in their hospital stay . . . I've managed to get to know the staff much better. I feel like part of the team there now . . . I am realizing that . . . pastoral authority in not built simply of whether I'm liked or perceived to be needed.

These brief examples illustrate the significant and profound growth each resident experienced in response to pastoral assignment change as reflected in the clinical rhombus. Their evaluation of the learning is *confirmed* by the statistics which show increased productivity and balance in their ministry. The energy and productivity in the group process has been enriched in a parallel manner.

Parallel Administrative Changes

The day after final evaluations, department directors at MMC were called to an administrative meeting. At this meeting, administrative chart changes were made for all department directors throughout the hospital. As director of the Department of Pastoral Care, Carole was notified by the executive director of the medical center, her administrator for the previous five years, that the department would now be reporting to an assistant administrator. Metaphorically, the administrative corner (A) of the clinical rhombus was being changed. Initially, she approached the meeting with feelings of shock, self-blame, and anger, much like the residents felt at the changes that had occurred for them. Through the fog of her own reaction, she became aware that these changes impacted every director and assistant administrator in the medical center. It was also apparent that many people had as little time to process these changes as she had.

In the day that followed this meeting, Carole reflected on the parallels of this change with the pastoral assignment changes. This raised the possibility that, while the methodology had been

The Clinical Rhombus Revisited

different, the actual changes might have parallel results and benefits for the directors, departments, and administrators of MMC.

Several events helped reinforce the parallel and challenged us as a department to move creatively beyond our initial resistance and blame. First, a number of people spoke to Carole, expressing similar feelings of loss, self-recrimination, and anger. Second, Logan reminded Carole that she had discussed with him possible transitions in administrative structure for our department as early as the fall of 1990. Finally, the pastoral care secretary helped by sharing general employee reactions to and assumptions regarding the administrative changes. The general employee (non-management) group had a less reactive response to the transitions and the timing, and this proved helpful in raising our objectivity in the midst of the subjective experience.

These three factors, combined with the recent work of the residents in assessing their own learning after the pastoral assignment changes, led us to create a new vision for the organization and management of our pastoral care department. The primary impetus for this actually came from the executive director as he talked with Carole prior to the administrative change. In his view, daily operations needed the more immediate attention of an assistant administrator, while the overall hospital and church-related concerns would be continued with the executive director. From this catalyst, we revised and redefined our ministry and responsibilities. Carole could now more freely relate to the hospital's Foundation in regard to the administration of the Golden Cross Endowment, and the promotion of the Future Fund, an endowment program driven by employee support. She needed to commit more time to the relationship with the church's annual conference and its relationship to the hospital by developing education for local church clergy and laity and to accept conference responsibilities for committee and board work. Logan's functions would be strengthened by the change in the administrative chart as he increased his accountability for daily operations, including budget, personnel, ministry in the hospital, management of our CPE program, and medical center programs such as advanced directives.

A further clarification within our working as a team came as we incorporated Kathy, the pastoral care secretary, more intentionally into her responsibilities for budgeting and office management.

With this revisioning for our future ministry, a transformation in our response to the administrative changes began to take place. Among the benefits of this process for our ministry was an increased freedom to move into ministry with hospital staff (management and general employees) who were still feeling the shock waves from the transition. We were able to move through our own initial resistance to individually and corporately counsel, support, and speak to the resistance, and challenge others to create possibilities for the future of MMC.

Conclusion

The clinical rhombus remains in force in the teaching of pastoral care. As such, it is embedded in the overall system in the learning environment. A change in one part of the rhombus produces corresponding changes in the other parts. We realized this once again when we changed the P corner of the rhombus. We also realized it when the A corner was changed for our department. Hersey and Blanchard say, "An organization is an 'open social system,' that is, all aspects of an organization are interrelated; a change in any part of the organization may have an impact on other parts or on the organization itself. Thus a proposed change in one part of an organization must be carefully assessed in terms of its likely impact on the rest of the organization."[9]

As CPE supervisors, we all utilize the clinical rhombus intentionally and unintentionally. This case study served to heighten our awareness of the critical and creative possibilities of change in the rhombus for pastoral formation. The case study and our intentional reflection on the events served to facilitate and enable our own pastoral responsibilities within the larger institution of our training center. In pursuing this curriculum design, we unwittingly

---

9. Hersey and Blanchard, *Management of Organizational Behavior,* 170.

The Clinical Rhombus Revisited

fulfilled beyond our own expectation Donald Schön's assessment of the reflective practitioner:

> In a reflective conversation, the values of control, distance, and objectivity—central to technical rationality—take on new meaning. The practitioner tries, within the limits of his virtual world, to control variables for the sake of hypothesis—testing for transformation, and as he tests them, he inevitably steps into the situation. He produces knowledge that is objective in the sense that he can discover error—for example, that he has not produced the change he intended. But his knowledge is also personal, its validity is relative to his commitments to a particular appreciative system and over-arching theory. His results will be compelling only for those who share his commitments.[10]

We revisited the clinical rhombus and discovered once again that learning can indeed take place through resistance and change. Our residents learned that. We did as well. The rhombus continues to provide a conceptual and theoretical model for the learning environment. Reflection upon the different corners of the rhombus provides a rich arena for pastoral formation and learning the art of pastoral care.

---

10. Schön, *Educating the Reflective Practitioner*, 79.

4

A Teachable Moment—For the Both of Us

DON MISSED OUR FIRST supervisory session because of a funeral. Then he "forgot" our next two supervisory sessions. He somehow managed to confuse the date or the time, and then he would be quite contrite and apologetic about it. When I confronted him about his forgetfulness, he was stunned. How dare I not accept his sincere and heartfelt apologies? How dare I not forgive his forgetfulness? I mean, here was a charming, handsome, delightful young man who seemingly had his act together. He had the potential to go far up the church ladder on charm and good looks alone. In fact, he already begun his climb. Don was well-liked by his church. He was smooth, no doubt about it. Historically, he had always been able to charm his way out of his forgetfulness.

But not now. He couldn't believe it. He did not like my use of words like "resistance" and "avoidance." I had a sense of Don's fearfulness beneath his charm. I wondered what he was protecting. His charm was not working now. I challenged Don to look at his self—his identity and his ministry—beyond the charm. His forgetfulness set the stage for a teachable moment for the both of us.

Don used my challenge to delve into his self. He moved into rich moments of affective learning as he realized the positive and negative aspects of his charm and how that kept him from really knowing others, and his own self, on an intimate, feeling level. A significant part of his learning occurred as he confessed to me a dark secret that happened long ago. Here was part of what he was trying to protect: the human, fallible, ugly part of his self. As he told me this story, I listened. I heard the pain in his voice. I saw the burden he had been carrying in his tears. When he finished, he saw my tears and heard my words of care and forgiveness for him. He was stunned. How dare I not punish him for this great sin of his? How dare I offer him grace instead of judgment?

Oh, but there had been enough punishment and judgment in his life. Don taught me that. As I listened to his confession, I remembered my own parallel process. I recalled times when I sat in a chair across from my supervisor—fearful, broken, hurting, and hoping—and not knowing what would happen in that intimate, powerful moment. I remembered those supervisors who heard my confessions of dark secrets and great sins. I remembered those supervisors who listened to me in my pain, in my lostness, and gently and gracefully heard me. I remembered those supervisors who forgave me in their own ways, who loved me, confronted me, accepted me, and challenged me.

I learned about grace and the meaning of the Good News when someone listened to me. The listening was transformative in my life. Maybe the pastoral aspect of supervision gets lived out and incarnated when we remember our own parallel process as we supervise. I learned what it means to be a pastor when someone was pastor to me.

I hope Don learned something as well.

5

Descent into the Underworld
The Hero's Journey as a Model for Group Development

THE DEVELOPMENTAL PROCESS OF groups over time is well-documented. This process has been studied extensively since World War II in different settings and among different disciplines. Even the studies have been studied. What has emerged in the research is that the group developmental process, for the most part, is remarkably predictable. Groups move through the same stages and dynamics in the beginning, in the middle, and in the end of their lives. This is true if the group is a work team with a specific task, a psychotherapy group, or a group of clinical pastoral education (CPE) students learning about the art of pastoral care.

Below, I review this developmental process and offer another model or way of understanding the process. This model will be based on mythologist Joseph Campbell's journey of the hero as he articulates it in his classic work *The Hero with a Thousand Faces*.[1] The primary emphasis will be on the essential nature of conflict in the group process. As will be seen, the stage of conflict parallels Campbell's hero's descent into the underworld. Finally, I discuss

1. Campbell, *Hero*.

the implications of this model for the group pastoral supervision of CPE students.

A Brief Review of Group Developmental Process

Group development has been defined as "the maturity and degree of cohesion that a group achieves over time as members interact, learn about one another, structure relationships, and roles within the group."[2] As a group goes through this developmental process, theorists have used a variety of descriptions to talk about these concepts of maturity, cohesion, learning, relationships, and roles. Usually, this is done by giving a name to the different stages as they emerge during the group process. The actual names and number of defined stages vary among the different theorists. This naming of stages implies there is a predetermined, rigid process. This is not the case. Group development, while clearly predictable, is more fluid than linear, more mysterious than rigid, and more dynamic than static. While the use of stages to describe group development promotes understanding of the broader frameworks, room must be left for the subtle and not-so-subtle exceptions to the stages. Yet in spite of these differences, similarities abound.

In general, a group as a whole moves through a developmental sequence of four stages.[3] First, there is period of orientation or encounter. Here the issues of safety, inclusion, and acceptance are primary. These issues have to be attended to in order for the group to develop further. Second, there is time of dominance and conflict. This is the most difficult stage for group members and leaders alike. Individual members and the group as a whole struggle with scapegoating; resistance to authority grows; and rigidity of roles may set in. This stage must be worked through successfully if the group is to move on to more productive work and relationships. Third, the group moves into cohesiveness and productivity. Once the conflict is processed sufficiently, if not successfully, the group is

---

2. Mennecke et al., "Implications of Group Development," 526.
3. Hemenway, *Inside the Circle*, 110–11.

able to risk more self-disclosure. There is deeper intimacy. Morale is high. There is a clear sense of success in the group work. Fourth, the group must deal with consolidation and separation. The end is near. The group must make meaning out of the overall experience. The end of the group is anticipated. There is grief to acknowledge; there is loss to mourn.

In *Introduction to Group Dynamics,* Knowles and Knowles summarize the stages of group development put forth by eleven different theorists.[4] Their summary points to the similarities and differences in naming the different stages as well as differences in the number of stages. For example, Knowles and Knowles cite Bion's three famous stages of Flight, Fight, and Unite. Also noted are Tuckman's well-known stages: Forming—Testing and Dependence; Storming—Intragroup Conflict; Norming— Development of Group Cohesion; and Performing—Functional Role-Relatedness. These two schemes, particularly Tuckman's, continue to be used as a reference in the field. Other models of the stages of group development are found in Johnson and Johnson and in Napier and Gershenfeld.[5]

Scott Peck put forth one of the more interesting theories in recent years of group development. In *The Different Drum,* Peck, a popular psychologist and amateur theologian, offers a four-stage process of group development based loosely on Bion's work.[6] The stages are (1) pseudocommunity, (2) chaos, (3) emptiness, and (4) community.

In the first stage of pseudocommunity, the group simply tries to fake it. Members are overly polite, almost to a fault. Accommodation to the other is the unspoken norm. Everyone gets along fabulously. On the surface, it looks as if real community has happened quickly and easily. It seems too good to be true. Of course, it is. In this stage, members withhold the truth from each other. Conflict is avoided at all cost. Feelings are kept inside for fear of

---

4. Knowles and Knowles, *Introduction to Group Dynamics,* 72.

5. Johnson and Johnson, *Joining Together,* 30; and Napier and Gershenfeld, *Groups, Theory and Experience,* 63–101.

6. Peck, *Different Drum,* 86–106.

offending someone. Becoming a group, Peck says, "requires time as well as effort and sacrifice."[7] In pseudocommunity, there has not been enough time for a real community to develop; neither has there been effort or sacrifice.

As the pseudocommunity wears thin, chaos, which has been lurking in the wings, finally emerges. For Peck and others, chaos is an essential part of the group development. It may be the most essential part. Usually chaos centers around a member's attempt to heal, convert, or control the others. Individual differences come out of hiding and into the open. There is no longer a way to avoid offending someone. This is a time of fighting and struggle, usually within the group and, more often than not, with the leader. It is an unsettling and uncomfortable time in the group. Peck suggests there are two ways out of chaos for a group. One way is through organization. That is, a member tries organizing the group through the assigning of tasks and roles to different members. This keeps the conflict at bay, and the emotional content contained. It keeps the process in the head, or intellectualized, rather than moving down into the heart, or into the affective dimension. The group then stays in pseudocommunity. The other way out is through emptiness.

Emptiness, for Peck, is the bridge between chaos and community. By emptiness, he means the emptying of the self's barriers to communication with the other group members. This means giving up expectations and preconceptions, prejudices, ideologies and theologies, and solutions. It means relieving oneself of the need to heal, convert, fix, or solve. It means, for the most part, giving up the need to control. This is incredibly difficult work. Peck suggests the process of emptying is much like dying. The person's transformation from an individual who happens to be in a group to a group member means there is a sense of loss. There is no way to avoid this if true emptying is to occur. However, the joy and satisfaction that come by being in a real community, by being part of a real community, temper this sense of loss.

---

7. Peck, *Different Drum*, 88.

The stage of community in Peck's model parallels Bion's "Unite" stage or Tuckman's "Performing" stage. The task is completed. The work is done. The anticipation of the end and the need for a good good-bye moves to the forefront. In community, there is high group morale. A deep and abiding understanding of the other emerges where there is room for the individual and for the group as a whole. For Peck, community represents life lived in the abundance of deep joy and deep sorrow, where all of life is felt more intensely. It becomes a spiritual, and even a mystical, experience.

However, not all groups end "happily ever after." This is important to remember in group development. Groups do fail to achieve community. Groups do fail to be productive. Some groups do stay mired in pseudocommunity unwilling to move into chaos. Groups do get stuck in chaos and are unable to move on to the other stages or recycle through them over and over again. In fact, Yalom suggests that the evidence of a sequential pattern of group development across time is weak at best.[8] As a caveat, he writes, "Thus, the boundaries between phases are not demarcated, nor does a group permanently graduate from one phase."[9] Simply put, the process of group development is paradoxical; it is predictable and mysterious, sequential, and dynamic. Such is the nature of the beast—the group.

The Descent into the Underworld

The journey of the hero is a universal, archetypal theme. It is found in all of the world's literature and mythology. In its essence, the hero is an individual who undertakes a journey, which, like the process of group development, is predictable in its sequences of events and stages. Campbell describes it thus, "A hero ventures forth from the world of common day into a region of supernatural wonder: fabulous forces are there encountered and a decisive victory won: the hero comes back from this mysterious adventure

---

8. Yalom, *Theory and Practice*, 303.
9. Yalom, *Theory and Practice*, 303.

Descent into the Underworld

with power to bestow boons on his fellow man."[10] One only has to think of persons such as Jason, Odysseus, Jesus, Parsifal, Buddha, and Luke Skywalker to see the universal nature of the journey. While Campbell's work, originally published in 1949, focused on male archetypes, I would suggest female heroes could be named as well. I think of Joan of Arc and Mother Teresa as two examples.

The parallels between the hero's journey and group development are striking. Thus, another model of group development can emerge using language and descriptions of this journey. Campbell sees the journey of the hero as consisting of a three-part cycle: (1) call and departure, (2) initiation or descent into the underworld, and (3) return.[11] The similarities between this cycle and Peck's model of group development are evident.

In Campbell's model, the hero is first called to an adventure. The call, Campbell suggests, "signifies that destiny has summoned the hero and transferred his spiritual center of gravity from within the pale of his society to a zone unknown."[12] Nothing will ever be the same again. The call of the hero is similar to the beginning of a group. The individual, for whatever reason, joins a group. He or she may be invited or assigned to a group. Membership in the group may either be required or voluntary. No matter, the individual is now faced with the task of how to be a part of the group. There are relationships to negotiate, tasks to perform, and decisions to be made about taking risks and being vulnerable. The individual has to decide at what level to participate and engage. In other words, will he or she be a leader or a follower? This is part of the call. In short, the call represents the initial movement into the unknown. Just as a group tries to fake it in the stage of pseudocommunity, the hero may try to fake responding to the call. But since the hero's spiritual center of gravity has moved into the unknown, there can be no faking it. Effort and sacrifice are now required.

Just as a hero is called to an adventure, a person joining a group is likely to be called to life-changing adventure. As the call

10. Campbell, *Hero*, 30.
11. Campbell, *Hero*, 30, 245.
12. Campbell., *Hero*, 58.

unfolds, there is a protector who appears almost magically. The task of this protector is to help the hero along the way. The help may take the form of wisdom or guidance, or a weapon or a magic spell. Likewise, in its early stages, a group turns to its leader for help. The leader helps structure the group, set appropriate boundaries, manage the environment, and monitor issues of trust and safety. The protector is here at this point to help the hero cross the threshold of liminal space and move into the unknown. Likewise, the group leader helps the group, as a whole, cross the threshold of liminal space and enter into the chaos.

As with group development, this threshold of liminal space is the critical part of the hero's journey. Without crossing over the threshold and descending into the underworld, the journey is aborted. It cannot be finished. It cannot be completed. This threshold then represents the door to the stage of chaos. On the other side of the threshold is darkness and terror. The way is unknown and full of danger. Campbell writes, "The adventure is always and everywhere a passage beyond the veil of the known into the unknown; the powers that watch at the boundary are dangerous; to deal with them is risky; yet for anyone with competence and courage the danger fades."[13]

As the hero crosses the threshold and descends into the underworld, Campbell notes he is required to do battle with dragons or demons, and face threats of dismemberment or crucifixion. The hero may be abducted or even forced into the belly of the whale. What is required of the hero at this threshold and beyond is neither easy nor for the faint of heart. Group work is not for those who wish to avoid adventure. In a group this is indeed chaos. Feelings run high. Anger may be expressed. Tears may be shed. The fighting and struggling are real and may seem like a battle with a dragon. The depth of feelings may cause a person to believe she is indeed lost in the whale's belly. The only way out is through. The ease, comfort, and niceness of pseudocommunity are gone. The chaos cannot be avoided, nor can the battles be fought from the head; they are of the heart. Emptying is now required.

13. Campbell, *Hero*, 82.

Descent into the Underworld

The hero is required to descend to the depths of the underworld. It is only in the depths where the gifts of the gods can be received. The gift cannot be received in the shallows. The gift is bestowed as a result of the ordeal of descent. Likewise, in a group, growth, learning, and transformation only come as the group as a whole moves through the chaos into the emptiness and then into community. This is the hard, difficult work of a group. Campbell puts it like this, "The agony of breaking through personal limitations is the agony of spiritual growth."[14] If the group stays stuck in pseudocommunity, then there are none of the benefits. If the hero does not respond to the call, then he will never receive the gift.

Once the hero receives the gift, the final work is that of return. The hero now returns to the known world. This return is much like the ending work required of a group. The task has been completed, the reward gained. For the group, now is the time to say good-bye. The hero has been changed by her descent into the underworld, and the group has been changed as well by its descent into and through chaos and emptiness.

The return to the known world is a time to celebrate. Often it may be simply a celebration of survival. Equally true, it may be a time of deep satisfaction and pride about achievements made, gifts received, and battles won. For a group, to return to the known world means there is recognition of being in a community where understanding and compassion are the norm, where intimacy is fostered, and where individuality is respected. The journey is now complete.

Implications for Clinical Pastoral Education

As a supervisor of clinical pastoral education, I teach students the art of pastoral care. CPE is professional education for ministry. Students learn about the art of pastoral care through the actual practice of ministry to persons while under the supervision of a certified CPE supervisor. They learn about ministry by doing

---

14. Campbell, *Hero*, 190.

ministry. A peer group experience provides a significant part of the curriculum. It is in the group process where students learn both to provide pastoral care and to reflect upon and evaluate that care.

Much of the students' learning and growth in CPE occurs in the group process. The group provides support, nurture, confrontation, clarification, and challenge. As the students are faced with intense crisis situations in ministry, they discover their own grief is touched and felt deeply. As they learn to listen to the pain and sorrow of the other, they learn to listen to their own. The group then becomes the container in which these feelings are processed and explored.

As the supervisor, or leader, I am required to be aware of the group dynamics at play. That is, I pay attention to the issues surrounding the call to adventure of the group. The ever-present issues of inclusion and safety are addressed. Often, it seems, groups of seminary students move rather quickly into pseudocommunity. Everyone likes one another. Everyone gets along so well with each other. It can be so sweet it is sickening. But the call to cross the threshold into chaos cannot be avoided for long. Grief and pain surface. Doubts and questions come out of the shadows. Tears, long held back, spill over. Anger, often cloaked under a pious version of Christianity, explodes. This is indeed the descent into the underworld for these students. They begin to discover that the descent does not destroy them, nor does it destroy the patients and family members they encounter. On the contrary, they discover that paradoxically the descent into the underworld is healing. Just as the hero has to battle dragons, the CPE students battle with their own feelings and their understandings of faith.

As supervisor, it is not my place to rescue the students from this descent into the underworld. I have been there. I know what it is like. I know how terrifying it can be. I know courage is needed. I know someone needs to point the way through. I also know no one can descend for the students. They must do it themselves. Thus, my role is to guide and guard the process. I want to help the students move from pseudocommunity and respond to the call to descend.

I want to provide the safety and trust to allow them to enter into the chaos and conflict. I seek to help contain the feelings of agony as they experience the breaking of personal limitations so there can be spiritual growth. I want them to receive the gift from God. I guide them in the return to the known world. I lead them into saying good-byes and celebrating their accomplishments. I desire to help them speak their truths and experience intimacy with each other. I know I cannot do the work for them. I can only guide, encourage, and challenge them in their efforts and sacrifices.

The group process in CPE invites students to turn inward and downward to move from the head down toward the heart, to descend and receive in order to be able to give back. James Hillman says, "If we discover the place of the soul—and the experience—of God to be darkly within and below, we must reckon with a perilous voyage."[15] Students do not undertake this perilous journey alone. As a CPE supervisor, I stand with the students as witness to the value of the journey. "To teach," as Laurent Daloz says, "is to point the way through the fire."[16]

---

15. Hillman, *Insearch*, 49.
16. Daloz, *Effective Teaching and Mentoring*, 237.

6

A Prayer for Healing Denied

THE CALL CAME FROM the pediatric ICU.

The nurse said a young girl was dying. She was five, maybe six years old. I don't remember other details. The parents wanted to see the chaplain. That was me. I was the on-call chaplain that night. It was snowing outside. It was a heavy snow. The flakes were large and peaceful. Solitude covered the land and my heart. I remember that it was quiet throughout the hospital.

The parents were hurting so bad. Their daughter was dying. There was no further medical treatment available. They wanted me to pray for a miracle of healing. A prayer was all that they had left, just a simple prayer for a miracle that their daughter would be healed and live. It was not too much to ask.

But I could not pray for healing that night.

See, I knew too much; or at least I thought I did at the time. I was immersed in Divinity School and taking a basic unit of CPE. This was before we morphed Basic CPE into Level I CPE. I was steeped through and through in the historical-critical methodology of the academy's imperial theology. I read Von Rad, Bultmann, Davies, and Barrett. I studied Brown, Käsemann, and Sanders. I bought this theology hook, line, and sinker. There was no other critical purchase indicated. It was all neat and correct: miracles had been debunked; healings were passé. All that was missing was compassion.

I could have prayed for a lot of things that night, but not for healing. It was better and safer to be theologically correct than to feel the depths of all the pain. It was easier to be theologically rigid than to admit to my helplessness. I was more interested in helping the parents through their denial and on toward acceptance. I knew my Kübler-Ross. I was learning clinical theory. My theology and interventional theory may have been right, but they were ever-so empty.

The parents asked me to leave. They would call someone else to come to the hospital to pray with them.

I do not know if this little girl was healed. I do not know if she lived or died.

But I do know that now when I pray for healing—and forgiveness—I pray for me.

7

You Learn It in Your Heart
Transformative Learning and Clinical Pastoral Education

WHEN MY DAUGHTER, KATIE, was nine years old, we talked about school at supper one night—hers and mine. She was in the fourth grade. I was taking a class in adult education at North Carolina State University in Raleigh, NC. After we talked about math, social studies, and the student council, I told her I was writing a paper for my class.

"What's it about?" she asked.

"It's about transformative learning theory," I said.

"Wow. That sounds good," she said, "but I have no idea what you are talking about."

"I bet you do. What does transformation mean?"

"It means a change," she said. She paused. "A really big change."

"That's right," I said. "When have you learned something that caused you to change?"

"Oh. Do you mean like learning something from a mistake?"

"Well, sure," I said. "How do you learn from a mistake?"

"Well, you have to think about it really hard, and then," she continued, "you will remember not to make the mistake again."

"That's exactly right. You have to think really hard about it. Now let me ask you this. When you learn something after thinking about it really hard, do you think you learn it in your head or in your heart?"

"You learn it in your heart," she said.

"See, Katie. You do know something about transformative learning theory, don't you?"

She beamed. "I guess I do," she said.

Not only does learning in your heart describe transformative learning theory, it is also an apt description of the learning process in CPE. Students in CPE are challenged on several different fronts: hard encounters with the living human documents in crisis situations, a strange methodology, an unfamiliar curriculum, a difficult group process, and an unsettling process of individual supervision. The learning is intense emotionally, often accompanied by tears, anger, and frustration, even laughter. The learning process is often disruptive, chaotic, and disorienting. Students and supervisors know this all too well. Formed in the discipline of adult education, transformative learning theory offers a fresh look at the learning process. It provides a theoretical basis for a new understanding of the change that many students experience in CPE.

Transformative Learning Theory

Professor Jack Mezirow of the Teachers College of Columbia University first proposed the theory of transformative learning in 1975 in a landmark qualitative research study of adult women who returned to community college to continue their education after a long absence.[1] As developed by Mezirow, transformative learning theory is a comprehensive theory of adult learning. It is a theory about how persons understand and interpret the many varied experiences which make up their lives and worlds in which they live. "A defining condition of being human," writes Mezirow, "is that we have to understand the meaning of our experience."[2]

1. Mezirow, *Education for Perspective Transformation*.
2. Mezirow, "Transformative Learning," 5.

As human beings, we are continually making meaning out of what happens to us and around us. We seek to make sense of the world and how it works. To that end, we have learned over time to construct a certain way of seeing and understand the world. We all have particular ways in which we interpret what occurs. Our ways of making meaning and seeing the world are grounded in unexamined values, beliefs, and assumptions. These values, beliefs, and assumptions are absorbed—often uncritically—from our families, communities, and cultures. Thus we all live with a set of expectations about how the world works and what it means. These expectations act as a lens through which the world and how we live and move and have our being is viewed.

But what happens to us when something occurs that does not fit into these expectations of the world? What happens when the unexpected occurs and our past experiences and all of our values, beliefs, and assumptions no longer help us make meaning? What happens when our world is turned upside down and inside out and we are disoriented? Students entering CPE are often unprepared for what they experience. Encounters with the "living human documents," with deaths, traumas, and codes, with peers in the group and with supervisors are challenging. Students are off-balance and reeling emotionally and spiritually. We basically have two main options when we experience the unexpected. The first option is to simply reject the unexpected through denial, repression, or some other coping mechanism, and thus hold fast to our familiar values, beliefs, and assumptions. The second option is to open ourselves up to begin the process of critically questioning and reflecting upon our unexamined expectations. Patricia Cranton writes, "When people critically examine their habitual expectations, revise them, and act on the revised point of view, transformative learning occurs."[3]

At its core, transformative learning theory is elegantly simple. It is about change. In broad terms, transformative learning is a process in which persons question, examine, validate, and reconstruct their perspectives on the world and the way it works. The theory

3. Cranton, *Understanding and Promoting*, 19.

seeks to understand the process by which a person's meaning perspective, or frame of reference, is changed as a result of encountering different perspectives and experiences.[4] Reflecting critically on these differing perspectives and reassessing one's beliefs, values, and feelings is vital to the process of transformation. This change in a person's frame of reference represents learning. Transformative learning theory suggests that when a person changes his or her frame of reference, that frame of reference typically becomes "more inclusive, discriminating, open, reflective, and emotionally able to change."[5]

As transformative learning theory has developed over the past 30-plus years, it has generated much conversation within the discipline of adult education. Several different perspectives of the theory have emerged in the literature.[6] These perspectives encompass a wide range of scholarship and practice, and further suggest that the theory is dynamic, unfolding, and, as Mezirow and his associates suggest, a work in progress. This paper will give a brief overview of the theory, focusing primarily on the rational and affective dimensions within the transformative learning process.

The Rational Dimension of Transformative Learning

Mezirow's conceptualization of transformative learning begins with his emphasis on perspective, or the way a person sees and makes sense of the world. A perspective is essentially a worldview, a lens through which experience is interpreted in order to make sense of and understand the world the person inhabits. Using Habermas's concept of emancipatory learning where learning is more than technical and practical, Mezirow defines a meaning perspective as "the structures of psycho-cultural assumptions within which new experience is assimilated and transformed by

---

4. Cranton, *Understanding and Promoting*; Mezirow, *Transformative Dimensions*; and Mezirow et al., *Learning as Transformation*.

5. Cranton, *Understanding and Promoting*, 23.

6. Merriam et al., *Learning in Adulthood*; and Taylor, "Making Meaning."

one's past experience."[7] A perspective transformation is a "process of becoming critically aware of how and why the structure of psycho-cultural assumptions has come to constrain the way we see ourselves and our relationships, reconstituting this structure to permit more inclusive and discriminating integration of experience and acting upon these new understandings."[8] In other words, a meaning perspective is represented by a person's predisposition to see life and experience it in a certain way. For example, a person may have certain expectations about the way a liberal Christian is supposed to think and act; or how a suburban soccer mom is supposed to vote; or how a Southerner is supposed to talk. These expectations are learned. They are socially, culturally, and personally constructed over time.

But as is well-known, life never stays the same. Change happens. Some of the change is due to the normal, everyday development and growth of the person. Other change occurs through cataclysmic and disorienting events. Mezirow suggests that when events and experiences do not fit into the person's already constructed and comfortable meaning perspectives, a sense of dissonance results. The world does not make sense. Events and experiences do not fit in the usual categories or frames of reference. In other words, out-of-the-norm experiences cannot be resolved within the usual perspectives. Something else is needed. Here, then, is the opportunity for questioning, reassessment, and change in perspective. Assumptions may be challenged. Questions may be raised. The old ways of seeing the world no longer seem to work. The new event does not fit in with the old meaning perspective. Transformation awaits. "When a meaning perspective can no longer comfortably deal with the anomalies in a new situation," Mezirow notes, "a transformation can occur."[9]

Mezirow's understanding of the transformative learning process came to include concepts like frame of reference, habits of

---

7. Mezirow, "Critical Theory," 6.
8. Mezirow, "Critical Theory," 6.
9. Mezirow, "Perspective Transformation," 104.

mind, and points of view.[10] A frame of reference includes cognitive, affective, and conative dimensions, and consists of two parts: habits of mind and points of view. A habit of mind is a "set of assumptions, broad, generalized, orienting predispositions that act as a filter for interpreting the meaning of experience."[11] Habits of mind provide ways of seeing the world and are grounded in life history, experiences, culture, and personality. In addition to habits of mind, a frame of reference also includes points of view, which are "set(s) of immediate, specific beliefs, feelings, attitudes, and value judgments."[12] A point of view is essentially the rules a person uses—often unconsciously—to interpret experiences. Moreover, Mezirow is cognizant how resistant to change meaning perspectives can be. As D. Stephenson Bond notes, ". . . in practice, challenges to deeply held convictions are generally met with bitter resistance."[13]

For Mezirow, the role of critical thinking is the most crucial element in the transformation process. Critical thinking drives the transformation of a person's frame of reference. For Mezirow, this means becoming aware of how we are caught up, often without even knowing it, in our own histories, psychological assumptions, and cultural presuppositions.[14] While emphasizing the importance of critical thinking, Mezirow also notes that frames of reference do not just consist of thoughts. Without going into detail, he suggests that meaning perspectives and frames of reference also have dimensions of feeling and will. While Mezirow does acknowledge there is a place for feelings and emotion with the process of transformation, he places more emphasis on critical thinking and its companions, reason and rationality.[15] Nevertheless learning through transforming one's frame of reference is more than simply acquiring new information and new skills, and in this way it is

10. Mezirow et al., *Learning as Transformation.*
11. Mezirow, "Learning to Think," 17.
12. Mezirow, "Learning to Think," 18.
13. Bond, *Archetype of Renewal,* 41.
14. Mezirow, "Transformative Learning as Discourse," 58–63.
15. Mezirow, "Learning to Think," 3–33.

different from instrumental learning. It requires a critical awareness of reflection on one's life history and the many cultural and psychological assumptions that shape his or her world.

Mezirow further suggests that the transformation of a frame of reference includes certain phases and processes. Based on Mezirow's original 1975 study, Cranton noted the transformative process included ten phases and processes:

- Experiencing a disorienting dilemma
- Undergoing self-examination
- Conducting a critical assessment of internalized assumptions and feeling a sense of alienation from traditional social expectations
- Relating discontent to the similar experiences of others—recognizing that the problem is shared
- Exploring options for new ways of acting
- Building competence and self-confidence in new roles
- Planning a course of action
- Acquiring the knowledge and skills for implementing a new course of action
- Trying out new roles and assessing them
- Reintegration into society with the new perspective.[16]

Mezirow suggests that the presence of a disorienting dilemma, the first of the ten phases, most often serves as a catalyst for a perspective transformation. Such a dilemma might be a life-changing event such as the death of a spouse, an unexpected divorce, the sudden loss of a job, or the diagnosis of a life-threatening illness. He says, "The traumatic severity of the disorienting dilemma is clearly a factor in the establishing the probability of a transformation."[17] The disorienting experience propels the person to begin the process of examining, questioning, and reflecting on his or her assumptions, values, beliefs, and understanding of the world. Transformative

16. Cranton, *Understanding and Promoting*, 20.
17. Mezirow, "Critical Theory," 7.

learning can also occur more gradually over time. There may be a slower, incremental change that occurs in a person's point of view which can eventually lead to a change in a habit of mind. This is certainly a familiar process in CPE for both students and supervisors.

For Mezirow, the transformative learning process is driven by rational discourse and critical reflection. These are two key elements found throughout Mezirow's writings on transformative learning. The rational process of discourse is essential for transformative learning, according to Mezirow. Rational thought and reasoning are primary and he provides a list of seven ideal conditions which should be met in order for habits of mind to be examined and questioned.[18] While Mezirow acknowledges that these conditions cannot be fully realized, he suggests they are important nonetheless. Persons in a transformative process involving a rational process of discourse will:

- Have accurate and complete information
- Be free of coercion and distorting self-perception
- Be able to weigh evidence and assess arguments objectively
- Be open to alternative perspectives
- Be able to reflect critically on perspectives and their consequences
- Have equal opportunity to participate
- Be able to accept an informed, objective consensus as valid.[19]

In addition to rational discourse, the practice of critical reflection drives the process of questioning assumptions and frames of reference and anchors transformative learning. Reflection brings into awareness unarticulated dynamics related to habits of mind. It is a conscious, rational process which seeks to consider experience through reason. It is an intentional cognitive activity.

18. Mezirow, "Understanding Transformation Theory," 222–32.

19. Mezirow, *Transformative Dimensions*, 78; and Cranton, *Understanding and Promoting*, 24.

In summary, several key elements frame the rational dimension of transformative learning theory: a central focus on a person's frame of reference, the how and why that frame of reference might be changed through questioning assumptions and presuppositions through critical reflection and rational discourse, a ten-phase process leading from a disorienting dilemma to a reintegration of a new frame of reference, and finally, an understanding that transformation may occur suddenly or over time. Cranton summarizes these elements in her summary of transformative learning:

> Transformative learning is defined as the process by which people examine problematic frames of reference to make them more inclusive, discriminating, open, reflective and emotionally able to change. It can be evoked by a single event—a disorienting dilemma—or it can take place gradually and cumulatively over time. Discourse is central to the process. We need to engage in conversation with others in order to better consider alternative perspectives and determine their validity.[20]

The Affective Dimension of Transformative Learning

While Mezirow's conceptualization of transformative learning emphasizes rational thought and discourse, there is more to the learning process than just cognitive endeavors. One of the primary critiques of Mezirow is that there is an over-reliance on rationality. Research suggests that more attention needs to be given to the significance of the affective dimension of transformative learning.[21] That is, what is the impact of emotions and feelings on the process of transformation? To explore this question means that one needs to look through different lens and attend to different dynamics in the learning process. The transformative learning theory literature suggests that there are three primary aspects of the affective dimension: grief, soul, and authenticity.[22] Underpinning these three

---

20. Cranton, *Understanding and Promoting*, 36.
21. Dirkx, "Power of Feelings," 63–72; and Dirkx, "Engaging Emotions," 15–26.
22. Boyd and Myers, "Transformative Education," 261–84; Cranton and

aspects and anchoring the theoretical conceptualization is Jungian psychodynamic theory with its emphasis of self and the concept of individuation.

Robert Boyd and Gordon Myers offer a different understanding of adult education and transformation than that of Mezirow. For them, transformation is geared toward ". . . the expansion of consciousness and the working toward a meaningful integrated life as evidenced in authentic relationships with self and others."[23] Transformation is driven by more than the rational and reasonable. In this conceptualization, transformation occurs through a process of discernment and grief work that is based in Jungian psychological theory. Concepts such as archetypes, shadow, persona, and self are essential to understanding what Boyd and Myers call transformative education. Transformative education is more focused on contemplating the integrative wholeness of life rather than rationally discussing and reflecting on experiences. Simply put, the process of discernment for Boyd and Myers centers on how a person becomes aware of his or her self in the world. The increase in self-awareness is critical to transformation here. To become and be a self, one must become aware of one's view of the world and how the world works.

Furthermore, Boyd and Myers suggest grief is the predominant condition for transformation. Grief is a natural process and reaction to change, especially when significant life events are involved. Grief is a normal and healthy process. Any change includes, at some level, a sense of loss. Therefore, grief is part of the change. When the world changes, grief is the appropriate, necessary, and often unwelcomed feeling. When disorientation strikes and there is disruption of the unexamined order of the world, grief is surely present and found in the resulting "bitter resistance." CPE students learn this in many different ways and through many different experiences. "Through grief work," write Boyd and Myers, "the individual searches out meaning based on their expanding

---

Carusetta, "Developing Authenticity," 276–93; and Dirkx, "Nurturing Soul," 79–88.

23. Boyd and Myers, "Transformative Education," 261.

consciousness and Self."[24] By situating transformation within the crucible of grief rather than critical thinking, Boyd and Myers present a radically different understanding of transformation. The grief process is central to the affective dimension of transformative learning.

Sue Scott likewise argues that the process of grieving is integral to transformation. Following Boyd and Myers, Scott reiterates that "transformation is not a rational process."[25] She argues that the affective dimension of transformative learning allows for the transformation to occur on a feeling level through images and symbols. For Scott, attending to the process of grieving is the core of transformative learning. What grief changes for a person is more complex than can be captured with rational thought. As six-year-old Amy said in a children's bereavement group, "Grief is complicated." Edward Edinger in his book on a psychological approach to the Psalms put it this way:

> Experience teaches us that psychological encounters with death, loss, grief, with sorrows of all kinds—when consciously met and dealt with—lead to a deepening and enlargement of personality, to a harvest rather than a loss. The tears of sorrow are in fact psychological seeds which, when harvested, bring renewal and an increase of life on a new level.[26]

Attending to the dynamics of grief as a person struggles with change and loss in his or her understanding of the world and of his or her self is essential to the affective dimension of transformative learning.

A second important aspect to the affective dimension of transformative learning is the concept of soul. John Dirkx introduced the concept of soul into the transformative learning lexicon arguing that transformative learning involves much more than a technical and rational approach.[27] He counters Mezirow's reliance

24. Boyd and Myers, "Transformative Education," 279.
25. Scott, "Grieving Soul," 44.
26. Edinger, *Sacred Psyche*, 122.
27. Dirkx, "Nurturing Soul," 79–88; Dirkx, "Images," 15–16; Dirkx, "Power

on rationality by emphasizing that transformative learning also involves personal ways of knowing and so makes use of imagination, symbols, and emotions—what he calls soul. For Dirkx, soul "is more than a psychological attribute, more than attending to feelings in learning . . . Soul has to do with authenticity, connection between heart and mind, mind and emotion, the dark as well as the light."[28] With this focus on soul, transformative learning in the affective dimension fosters self-knowledge through the use of symbols, imagination, and emotions. Dirkx further acknowledges that adult learning is often chaotic. By grounding transformation in soul, he moves the theory out of the head and into the heart, to speak metaphorically. The use of soul in transformative learning provides another facet through which one can view the transformative learning process. Following Dirkx, Valerie Grabove suggests that transformative learning is "soul learning."[29]

Dirkx also argues that as an individual attends to the affective dimension, he or she will necessarily be concerned with emotions and feelings associated with a particular learning experience, and so becomes aware of his or her self which until this point may have been little more than an unconscious notion. According to Dirkx, self-knowledge often comes through symbolic experiences rather than through direct language, and that therefore the process of meaning making involves the recognition, naming, and elaboration of the different aspects of the self and its accompanying images and symbols.[30] This process of meaning making is what Jung called individuation.

Thus, Dirkx's conceptualization of adult learning sees emotion and imagination as integral in the process of meaning making. For Dirkx, the affective dimension of transformative learning necessarily includes emotions. Since emotions are central to the human experience, they should not be avoided in adult learning situations. Rather the emotional content of experiences needs to

of Feelings, 63–72; and Dirkx, "Engaging Emotions," 15–26.

28. Dirkx, "Nurturing Soul," 82–83.

29. Grabove, "Many Facets," 92.

30. Dirkx, "Power of Feelings," 63–72; and Dirkx et al, "Musings and Reflections," 123–39.

be embraced. It is through our emotions that we shift through and make meaning of those experiences. Emotions are critical to the process of meaning making. A person's understanding of his or her self is fundamentally grounded in an emotional understanding of the self. For Dirkx, emotionally charged experiences are to be approached. They are not to be avoided or denied as being inappropriate. Making meaning is more than a rational, ego-based experience. It involves the emotional, spiritual, and transpersonal elements of knowing. Dirkx regards "emotion as integral to the meaning-making process."[31] He notes, "Emotions always refer to the self, providing us with a means of developing self-knowledge. They are an integral part of how we interpret and make sense of the day-to-day events of our lives."[32] This is indeed the "soul work" of the affective dimension of transformative learning. The CPE process certainly fits into this description of learning.

The third aspect of the affective dimension of transformative learning is the concept of authenticity. A somewhat elusive concept in adult education, Cranton locates authenticity in Jungian psychodynamic theory.[33] For Cranton, authenticity is grounded in the process of becoming conscious, acquiring self-knowledge, and working towards individuation. She suggests that the process of becoming conscious, becoming aware of self and the world, is a central tenet of transformative learning theory. While Mezirow relies on rationality and critical thinking to convey the transformative process, Cranton turns to Jung. She writes, "From a Jungian perspective, becoming conscious involves examining the unexamined, becoming aware of depths of the Self, moving underneath the surface of life. It occurs through introspection, reflection, delving into our emotions and imagination."[34] Authenticity rests on more than rational thought. Authenticity calls for an understanding and awareness of one's emotional life, of the soul work Dirkx speaks about. The more a person becomes aware of his or

    31. Dirkx, "Engaging Emotions," 16.
    32. Dirkx, "Power of Feelings," 64–65.
    33. Cranton, "Jungian Perspective," 120–25.
    34. Cranton, "Jungian Perspective," 121.

her self in relation to others and the world, the more authentic that person will be in those relationships. Of course, the ACPE Standards speak to the importance of self-awareness in pastoral formation and pastoral competence.[35]

For Cranton, authenticity is found in self-knowledge, that is, knowledge of one's own life narratives. By gaining self-knowledge a person begins to critically question and reflect upon previously unexamined values and beliefs. Cranton holds that gaining self-knowledge leads to transformative learning. "Transformative learning," she writes, "depends on increasing self-knowledge."[36] The process of gaining self-knowledge is the Jungian process of individuation, a process by which a person becomes conscious and develops self-knowledge. Jung defined individuation as "the process by which individual beings are formed and differentiated; in particular, it is the development of the psychological individual as being distinct from the general, collective psychology. Individuation, therefore, is a process of differentiation, having for its goal the development of the individual personality."[37] In other words, individuation is a process by which a person becomes aware of who he or she is, and how he or she is different from others. It means becoming more fully conscious of one's self and of one's place in the world. It means becoming a more fully unique individual. Murray Stein notes that "the process of individuation requires questioning one's most cherished cultural certainties and dearly held convictions. Individuation means letting go of earlier identifications and being open to exploring what is unknown and often distasteful."[38] Since, for Cranton, the process of transformative learning is also a process of individuation, authenticity, individuation, and transformation are interlaced. Authenticity is then the genuine expression of the self in the context of a myriad of understandings of how the self relates to others and to the world.

---

35. ACPE, *Standards*, 10.
36. Cranton, "Jungian Perspective," 122.
37. de Laszlo, *Basic Writings*, 266.
38. Stein, *Principle of Individuation*, 202.

Not surprisingly, Cranton suggests that one of the primary facets of authenticity is self-awareness.[39] In the context of teaching, Cranton suggests that one's awareness of one's history and how one sees oneself as a teacher is critical. Genuine relationship with another person, the student, is predicated on such self-awareness. Just as self-awareness drives authenticity, so authenticity drives the ability to establish open and honest relationships with students. The process of authenticity models the process of transformation.

Conclusion

The affective dimension of transformative learning acknowledges that while transformative learning has a rational component, other facets are of equal importance. These other facets include recognizing the process of grief when any change occurs, being aware of soul as a metaphor for the deep learning called for by emotions and symbols, and finally, understanding that authenticity in transformative learning involves the emergence of the self. The affective dimension of transformative learning is situated in Jungian psychodynamic theory and as such understands transformation as paralleling the process of individuation. The self-awareness called for by the affective dimension of transformative learning is rooted in an understanding of the narratives of the individual's life and his or her relationships with self, others, and the world.

In the clinical pastoral education setting, transformative learning theory, with its particular emphasis on the affective dimension of learning, provides both CPE supervisor and student with a rich understanding of learning and change. The theory recognizes the power of the emotional aspects of the learning process, especially those of grief, soul, and authenticity. While there is significant emphasis on the rational dimension of the transformative learning process, there is much more to transformation. Transformation is more than cognitive change.

Katie had it right: "You learn it in your heart."

---

39. Cranton, "Fostering Authentic Relationships," 5–13.

8

A Psalmist

DAVE'S SERMON WAS AWFUL. It was an agony for our worship seminar to listen to it. While it was obvious he had worked hard on this sermon, it was still bad. Oh, to be sure, he had read a lot of commentaries and preaching books. That was clear. The sermon was full of quotes from the likes of Tillich, Craddock, and Willimon. But Dave himself was not in it. He was nowhere to be found.

Dave was in his first year of divinity school and serving as a student pastor of a small rural church. I experienced him as bewildered about preaching—and about ministry for that matter. He so badly wanted to "do it right," and to play the role of the preacher. As the unit unfolded, I saw that Dave was not sure how personal reflection and growth would enhance his ministry. I suspected this was his way of discounting what he had to offer to people. And so he seemed to be bound by all the academic considerations, the technical aspects of exegesis, the theology of others, and the hard work of sermon preparation. His sermon was still dry and lifeless. He was embarrassed. Mercifully, the tape finally ended.

We sat in silent relief and embarrassment for a few moments. Dave began to tell us there was more to him than what was revealed in the sermon. In his parish, he told, he would write a simple melody for the psalm in the responsive reading and teach the refrain to the congregation as he played the piano. Then they would pray and sing the psalm together.

I had a hunch then that this was what Dave really wanted to process. He wanted to reveal the depths of his soul to us through his music, not his preaching. With a little encouragement—he was embarrassed about his gift of music—Dave rewound the tape and played the responsive reading of the psalm. It was a beautiful, haunting melody, simple and yet full of passion, faith, and his soul. When it was finished, there were tears in his eyes, and in mine and those of his peers as well. The silence which filled the room this time was not embarrassment, but the fullness of the presence of God.

I invited Dave to create the psalm he would sing of his life. He became quiet and reflective, and then slowly he spoke of his hope that there would be light in his darkness, faith amidst his doubt, and blessing for his search for God. This was personal, alive; this was Dave. There was no exegesis now, no quotes from others, just a young pastor reaching into his experience and discovering what it means to be a psalmist in this broken world.

I don't imagine Dave will ever be a dynamic preacher. But I hope he learned that faith and hope—the Good News of the Gospel—are not only to be found in textbooks, commentaries, and quotes, but within his own self, within his own gifts, and within his own psalms. That is what he has to offer. I believe Dave will touch people's lives with his gift of music and his own psalms. I know he did mine.

9

PFM as a Standard of Practice

As I was reading through the "Standards of Practice for Professional Chaplains in Health Care Setting," I recalled an encounter I had with an emergency department nurse several years ago. I was working at Methodist Medical Center in Dallas, Texas, one of the three trauma centers in the city. The ED stayed in a constant churn with gunshot wounds, stabbings, car accidents, heart attacks, and the usual mix of the walking sick and the worried well. The chaplain interns and residents in the CPE program were fully integrated into the organization. They were routinely called to the ED to provide pastoral care and support to out-of-control families where there was wailing and gnashing of teeth, angry outbursts, and the rending of garments and furniture. It was intense, emotionally draining ministry, and these CPE chaplains often wondered if their presence made a difference. Did anyone notice? Was it worth the cost?

One afternoon I was making rounds. I was talking with a seasoned, savvy nurse about a case from the day before. I don't recall the specifics now. I do remember that she said the on-call chaplain came down when called, got the details, went into the room with this hysterical family, and worked his PFM.

"What?" I said. "What do you mean, PFM?"

The Care of Souls

The nurse was embarrassed. She realized what she had said. So she then sheepishly explained, "Oh, that's what we call it when you guys go into a room where there is all the crying and yelling. You go into the room and we have no idea what happens in there, no idea what's going on but something happens."

She continued, "We don't see it but the yelling stops. The crying slows down, people calm down . . . It's Pure Fucking Magic. You know, PFM. We don't know how you do it. We don't know what else to call it, except PFM."

I laughed. I got it and she got it.

What we do is indeed magical. Maybe that is what the standards are trying to say.

10

Men's Movement

THE CANCER SITS IN his chest, inching its way, waiting, ticking. "The docs can tell me in about six weeks if the radiation is working," Robert says. And so he waits. And he coughs.

He tells me over the next few weeks how he wants to make things right with the kids, but the chasm of estrangement is wide. The blasts of radiation take their toll and the fires of chemotherapy leave their mark. Robert's hair begins to fall out. It is not working. Then comes the unrelenting nausea. There are no words now for his despair, only vomit, then dry heaves. The sickness is in his soul. "Yea, though I walk through the valley of the shadow of death . . ." Robert is 41, my age. He tells me he wants to get right with the Lord, and then he asks me to do his funeral. He *moves* in and out of sleep. I hold his hand and pray. And when he dies, I honor his request.

* * * * * * * * *

I look at Mr. Thompson. His daughter says he is 83 years old. "He has had a full life," she says. Now his emphysema is choking him. He can't breathe; only a dark gasp escapes. His kidneys are shutting down and he is slowly being poisoned. All the wheels are coming off. His son tells the doctor, "Do everything you can. Do everything you can." I cringe. He will not be swayed nor *moved*. When is enough enough?

They leave. And so I stay. I watch. Mr. Thompson thrashes in the bed. Or is it a seizure? His arms are restrained and a moan fills the room. He kicks the sheets off, his eyes wide and wild. He grabs at his heart. Does it hurt? Is it breaking? When will this be over? When will welcome sleep come? Soon. Soon. "Father, into thy hands..."

* * * * * * * *

Michael is beaten down. The night sweats leave him wasted and hair pasted to his forehead. The Kaposi's sarcoma lesions scream out. The pneumocystis pneumonia slowly and surely strangles him. Shingles make every *movement* one of pain. There is no rest. There is no reprieve. There is no cure. He is defeated. The room is oppressive. It is hard to breathe. The world has gone into slow motion. I wish I knew what to say to him. Talking leaves him exhausted. I wonder who will scream for him. Will it be me?

Michael's mother hovers about, wanting to help but not knowing how. Her pain is matched by his. There is much to be said here, but awkwardness now reigns. The vigil continues until that morning when, at age 26, even before Mozart dies and sweet Jesus was set free, and an echo is heard, "Eli, Eli..."

* * * * * * * * *

Tommy is only 19. He has sliced his wrists deeply, maybe as deeply as his unspoken pain and despair. His father is angry and wishing he could have done more. "Why didn't I love him more?" he cries. "Why didn't I love him enough?" His mother sits on the floor and softly weeps. That morning the blood flowed out of Tommy, and into his family and friends flowed all the sorrow and anguish and anger and questions and hurt and bewilderment.

The note said something about hoping Jesus would forgive. Now they wait for the word they hope they will never hear, a word of finality, a word pronouncing death. There is no *movement* on the EEG. All is flat. His daddy kisses him goodbye and *moves* out into the night.

> *O God, in whom we live and move and have our being,*
> *Have mercy on us fathers and sons and husbands and brothers,*
> *Have mercy on us all.*

11

I Walk Through Life Oddly
Dispositions, Character, and Identity in Clinical Pastoral Supervision

SUPERVISION IN CLINICAL PASTORAL education (CPE) is a complex and multi-faceted endeavor. What might look simple on the surface becomes rather treacherous as the process unfolds. Just ask any person in the Association for Clinical Pastoral Education (ACPE) certification process. There are many factors to consider in the process; some are obvious like the position papers students preparing to be clinical pastoral supervisors are required to write, in which they state their emerging understanding of theology, personality, and education as related to supervisory practice. Other factors are not so obvious. These other factors, often operating on subterranean levels, impact the educational process. For example, the supervisor needs to know something about the context in which a particular CPE program occurs. The content of the curriculum needs to address the various levels and specific objectives and outcomes for the program. Power dynamics are always at play and need to be recognized. Ethical issues need to be addressed. The competing interests between service to the institution and the educational process for the students have to be acknowledged.

Both the informal and formal evaluation processes need to be put in place fairly. Learning goals need to be developed in accordance with current ACPE standards. Issues of safety and trust in the group and in individual supervision must be acknowledged and addressed. The minute details of program administration require attention. Issues surrounding the theology and practice of ministry need focus. All of these factors and more need to be addressed by the supervisor. The process of pastoral supervision, like peeling an onion, consists of many different layers, all of which make up the transformative experience of CPE.

Historically, the literature in CPE has focused primarily on theoretical developments in supervision. There is a void, however, when it comes to reflecting on curriculum planning and why we do what we do. For example, one will find only a smattering of articles on the theory and use of verbatims in our literature.[1] Wittingly or unwittingly, we still follow the outline of Russell Dicks from the mid-1930s.[2] Curriculum planning stays hidden in the background of CPE programs or gets lumped under the headings of "process education" and "clinical method of learning." How we plan a curriculum operates mainly on an implicit level in supervision. We do what we do because that is the way we were taught. We may have learned a certain way of doing verbatims, interpersonal relation seminars, individual supervision, and theological reflection, and so adopt that method as part of the curriculum. We may even branch out ever so slightly and use films and other media as a curriculum resource. Some supervisors stress the importance of quantitative research as part of the curriculum and others do not. In this essay, I offer some reflections on curricular planning as one particular aspect of the supervisory process.

In the field of adult education, there are many different and competing theories of program and curriculum planning. Current adult education theorists in the area of program planning include Stephen Brookfield, Rosemary Caffarella, Ronald Cervero

---

1. Jones, "Baptism by Fire," 125–42; and Nouwen, "Case-Recording," 1–11.
2. Cabot and Dicks, *Art of Ministering to the Sick,* 256–7.

and Arthur Wilson, Thomas Sork, and Jane Vella.[3] Each theorist offers a certain way of planning while acknowledging biases and assumptions embedded in the theory along with different emphases and different uses of language. For example, Brookfield emphasizes reflective practice in applying principles of adult education to the program planning process. His work seeks to bridge a high-level theoretical perspective with the everyday practicalities found in specific contexts. Like Brookfield, Caffarella seeks to integrate the theoretical concepts with practical knowledge. She proposes an intentional integrative model of program planning. Cervero and Wilson focus on moving program planning from technical rationality to recognition of the power dynamics operating in educational systems. Sork, on the other hand, brings to the fore an awareness of the ethical responsibility of the program planner. He argues that program planners need to recognize the moral commitments within the programs that are developed. Finally, Vella makes extensive use of dialogue, grounded in adult education theory, to facilitate the design of educational programs. The discipline of CPE has yet to reach a similar level of reflection on our own biases and assumptions which drive our educational methodology. I believe what is missing in these theories is any attention to the disposition and character of the adult educator. The disposition and character of the adult educator is crucial to the unfolding of the educational process. Since CPE places a strong emphasis on the use of self in the practice of supervision, reflection on the identity of the supervisor is essential. The disposition and character of the pastoral supervisor, in the final analysis, shape the CPE process.

Dispositions, Character, and Identity

A disposition is defined as a prevailing tendency or inclination. It might be described as a person's temperamental makeup, nature,

---

3. Brookfield, *Understanding and Facilitating*; Caffarella, *Planning Programs*; Cervero and Wilson, *Planning Responsibly*; Sork, "Planning Educational Programs," 171–90; and Vella, *Training Through Dialogue*.

and tendency to act in a certain way. For example, a person might be described as having a cheerful disposition. Students in a summer CPE program described one of their peers as "Mr. Sunshine." His understanding of ministry revolved around his attempts to cheer up patients even when they did not want to be. An individual whose reactive response to any suggestion is always a quick and critical "No" may be seen as a contrarian. Other persons could be seen as a joker, an eternal optimist, or a sad sack; others might be thought of as being hot-headed and aggressive or a soft-hearted romantic. Dispositions appear as moods or attitudes about life in general and reflect the qualities of an individual. In this way, dispositions push reflection back onto the issue of character.

In the adult education program planning literature, there are no references to how the dispositions of the educator might impact and influence the educational process. Much of the literature is focused on the theories to be learned and the skills to be mastered. More often, the concept of dispositions is referred to in the K-12 teaching literature where a person has, say, a disposition for science education or a disposition for teaching reading. The teacher is said to be inclined toward or have a temperament for this particular arena.

Colleen Aalsburg Wiessner takes this understanding of disposition as an inclination or temperament further as she defines dispositions as "values, attitudes, and commitment in action."[4] For Wiessner, dispositions are more about the character and identity of the educator than a predetermined set of skills like teaching reading, which might be developed and brought to bear on the educational process. Wiessner's language is echoed in Standard 309.2 of the ACPE. This objective speaks to how the ACPE center's curriculum is designed "to develop student's awareness of how their *attitudes, values, assumptions, strengths, and weaknesses* affect their pastoral care (italics mine)."[5] Wiessner's definition of disposition with its emphasis on action invites reflection on exactly *how* these values, attitudes, and commitments are experienced in

4. Wiessner, personal communication.
5. ACPE, *Standards*, 13.

the educational process. To wit: How are these values, attitudes, and commitments embodied within the educator and thus lived out in and during the educational program? What is the action needed in order to experience the person's values, attitudes, and commitments?

Character Matters

James Hillman's work on character is instructive here.[6] As an archetypal psychologist, Hillman describes character as a calling, the essence of the individual as it were. Character is the core identity found deep within an individual. According to Hillman, a person is "born with a character."[7] It is character that defines the person. Character challenges. Character will not let go. It is embedded in each person's calling. Character is what defines the person's life when they say, "I can do no other." Or yet, when the person says, "I can be no other." More: Hillman argues character is not just *what* I do; it is the *way* I do it. Character is what is embedded. Character is what is seen. I used to say to students that doing an overnight on-call shift in the hospital builds character. Now I tell them that it reveals character. Their character, their core identity, is revealed in the way they practice ministry in the deep of the night when no one else is watching. They see their character.

The concept of character defies rational conceptualization. For James Hillman, "character is mystery, and it is individual."[8] It cannot be reduced to data, studied, or quantified. Rather character may be seen, for example, as passion, as effort, as vision. It is the way a person's values and attitudes are embodied. For example, the character of the supervisor may be seen in the *way* the issue of safety is addressed, in the *way* students are respected, in the way dialogue is encouraged, and in the *way* power is acknowledged and used.

---

6. Hillman, *Soul's Code*; and Hillman, *Force of Character*.
7. Hillman, *Soul's Code*, 7.
8. Hillman, *Soul's Code*, 251.

The character of an individual is what the world sees and certainly what students see in supervision. They see and experience, often on an unarticulated level, the character of the supervisor. What most of us remember from our supervisors is not their theories or skill sets or how they planned a unit of CPE, but rather we remember who they were to us. We tell different stories of our encounters, stories of challenge, of humor, and maybe even of anger, maybe even of their weirdness. "Could you believe it when Supervisor X said . . . ?" We remember how we were listened to, encouraged, and pressed to do the hard interior work required by this process. It is their dispositions and character that make a difference in our lives, not their theories. As put in another ancient context, character is brought forth from within the supervisor in the educational process. It cannot be avoided. It is the authentic core that will be revealed. The paradox—and miracle—of the CPE process is that the way the supervisor brings forth their character in the supervisory relationship invites and challenges the student to do the same. This is another way of speaking about the use of self in the supervisory process.

James Hillman goes on to suggest that character eventually rests on differences. He notes that character is "an observable mark, quality or property by which any thing, person, species, or event may be known as different from something else."[9] In adult education, for example, there are distinct differences in the program planning models espoused by Brookfield and Cervano and Wilson. And Sork's model is different than Caffarella's. The differences are not just simply in how theory is formulated and in the skill set needed to implement it. There is more to it. The difference goes back to the character of each theorist and the way the values and attitudes are embodied. Pastoral supervisors are no different. The art of supervision arises from within. Furthermore, Hillman argues that rational, behavior-centered language cannot do justice to character. Poetic language is needed to describe what is embodied, what is seen and always on display. He says, "Character forces me to encounter each event in my particular style. It forces me to

---

9. Hillman, *Force of Character*, 98.

differ. I walk through life oddly. No one else walks as I do, and this is my courage, my dignity, my morality, and my ruin."[10] No one else supervises as I do for good and ill. Character is brought forth from within.

Whatever kind of CPE program is planned, the character of an individual supervisor points beyond the skills and issues needed to be addressed to something more essential: character points to the way the program is planned. Character does not settle for an analysis of the what. Character invites the supervisor to look deeper into the curriculum process and to look beyond or below issues, for example, of technicality and social-political dynamics.

Character and Identity

Not surprisingly therefore, character is intimately related to identity. Whereas Hillman says character is not *what* I do but rather the *way* I do it, Parker Palmer frames identity in a somewhat different manner. Palmer proposes that ". . . we teach who we are."[11] The implications of this statement for the use of self in the supervisory process are legion. Supervision is intimately connected to the curriculum planning process; it is neither an isolated endeavor nor is it done on the spur of the moment without thought. The supervisory process is woven into a solid curriculum planning process in which all the attendant issues are addressed. What is the primary focus and purpose of the verbatim? What is the intent of IPR? Why choose a certain set of readings over another? What is the most important thing a beginning CPE student needs to learn?

Good curriculum planning, like good supervision, is grounded in the total personhood of the educator—his or her dispositions, character, and identity. While Palmer insists, ". . . teaching . . . emerges from one's inwardness, for better or worse,"[12] I would suggest the same principle applies to the curriculum planning

10. Hillman, *Force of Character*, 181.
11. Palmer, *Courage to Teach*, 2.
12. Palmer, *Courage to Teach*, 2.

process. The process of planning emerges from the supervisor's sense of identity. Curriculum planning, like supervision, is not an isolated process unconnected from the supervisory event or, and this is the main point, the character of the supervisor.

Moreover, Palmer says that teaching is about creating the good conditions for learning. He writes, ". . . good teaching requires that we understand the *inner* sources of both intent and the act (italics mine)."[13] This is also true for the curriculum planning. Understanding the inner sources of the supervisor for planning is essential for good teaching. This knowing is more than being able to name a certain skill set. It is deeper and richer. It goes beyond simply following a theory to its logical conclusion. It is more complicated and more mysterious. Good curriculum planning comes out of a sense of identity. What are my strengths as a pastoral supervisor? What are my weaknesses? Where are my blind spots? Knowing one's identity is prior to and foundational for planning, and subsequently for good supervision. As a white, middle-aged, privileged male, I have learned—and been convicted—over the years about differences and diversity. In my bumbling ways, I learned there were other visions of pastoral care and theology than that of white males; there were other ways of seeing and understanding the world. My CPE curriculum these days includes, for example, not only Carroll Wise and John Patton but Carrie Doehring, Harriet Goldhor Lerner, and Edward Wimberly as well.

"Good teaching," Palmer insists, "cannot be reduced to techniques; good teaching comes from the identity and integrity of the teacher."[14] There is no other way. Similarly, good supervision cannot be reduced to techniques, however tempting that may be. Good supervision arises from the identity, character, and disposition of the supervisor. It is what is brought forth from within the teaching and learning encounter.

In sum, dispositions, character, and identity are intimately interrelated and connected to each other. They are not distinct, stand-alone concepts but they work hand-in-hand to provide an

13. Palmer, *Courage to Teach*, 6.
14. Palmer, *Courage to Teach*, 10.

image of personhood that is, as Hillman says, mysterious and individual.

Implications of Dispositions, Character, and Identity on Curriculum Planning

Dispositions, character, and identity constantly interact with all the issues involved in the supervisory process. This constellation of dispositions, character, and identity is at the core of teaching and foundational to the supervisory process. In the final analysis, pastoral supervision is more about the *who* rather than the *what* or the *how*. It is the *who* which really determines the *what* and the *how*.

If that proposal is correct, and I believe it is, then the morally primary question changes. Who am I as a pastoral supervisor and educator is still a critical question but there is more: How does my identity as a pastoral supervisor and educator impact my curriculum planning? Hillman and Palmer are clear. I do what I do because of who I am. I supervise because I am a pastoral supervisor, not the other way around. For example, I am a pastoral supervisor because I supervise. Becoming and being a pastoral supervisor is more than a role; it is a vocation, a summons, a calling. Some suggest a calling might even be destiny.[15] I supervise because I can neither do nor be any other. The moral primacy of dispositions, character, and identity calls for the supervisor then to be/become aware of the way his or her whole personhood gets embodied in the curriculum planning process.

There are, of course, many ways to supervise, and many values to commit to the supervisory endeavor, although the ACPE certification process may be in danger of unknowingly pressing supervisory students to be more alike than different. For instance, my own embodiment of identity will be different from another person's. My own dispositions, character, and identity show up in different strengths and different weaknesses. At this point in my life, I am being drawn into poetry. Poetry speaks to me now in

---

15. Meade, *Fate and Destiny*; and Hollis, *Creating a Life*.

I Walk Through Life Oddly

ways that are life-shattering. I find that there is emotional power in poetry. It provides a radically different engagement of experiences as it touches and conveys the emotional core of those experiences. Through an economy of words and the use of images and metaphors, poetry captivates the language of feelings. I find that poetry serves as a gateway into the emotional aspects of learning.[16] The emotional aspects of learning are transformative and are critical in the CPE process. Poetry helps me tap into that part of learning. Something from within is being called forth, often in odd and weird ways, as I even try to write poetry.

I now incorporate poetry into my curriculum in different ways. For example, I select a poem to begin a seminar session. I give each student a copy and I read it out loud in a *lectio divina* way. We do not discuss the possible meanings of the poem; rather my intent is to let the emotional power of the poem simply sit with each person however they hear it. It is not within my understanding to give them the exact meaning of the poem. I use poems by some of my favorite poets such as Mary Oliver, Rainer Maria Rilke, David Whyte, Wendell Berry, and Jane Hirschfield. I find that the themes of the poems I select—journey, grief, searching, love, nature, God—show up in the seminar work. Students are able to make connections between the poems and their struggle to learn the art of pastoral care. I write final evaluations using one of the poems as an extended metaphor for the student's learning process. I try to weave the words of the poet with a description of the learning and the ACPE outcomes. I ask the student to also pick one poem that has been most meaningful to them and most representative of their learning. It is a nice synchronistic feeling when we both choose the same poem. I have more passion and energy for writing evaluations in this manner, and it is more meaningful to me than a checklist. All in all, I find that poetry invites and challenges students to think differently, to see differently, to feel differently. Some poems speak to students on a profound level. Some students shake their heads, roll their eyes, and say they don't get it. Even as

---

16. Housden, *Ten Poems*.

I am writing this, I wonder about using music in this way. We all have our own odd and weird ways.

A focus on dispositions, character, and identity in the supervisory process requires an awareness of the diverse gifts and graces of each person. There simply is not a "one-size-fits-all" theory of pastoral supervision, just as there is not a single theory of curriculum planning and just as there is not a single set of dispositions which make for good planning. There are no "best-in-class" character values which lend themselves to superb supervision or planning. There is no one certain, set apart, and most desired identity for the ideal pastoral supervisor of CPE programs. Such a person does not exist, contrary to expectations years ago that supervisory students could write a paper about the ideal supervisor. The program planners in adult education are unique, each bringing their own gifts and oddities into the process. Each theorist beings his or her own strengths and weaknesses into the planning process along with his or her unique dispositions, character, and identity.

It should be noted here that while dispositions, character, and identity are at the core of the curriculum planning process, they are not static concepts. A supervisor's disposition, character, and identity are not once-for-all, set-in-stone, unchangeable, and therefore unable to be developed. Rather, I believe that dispositions, character, and identity can be shaped, nuanced, challenged, and called forth by intentional personal reflective work. Growth and learning do indeed occur for supervisors as well as students. There are two models for this development of an increased awareness of the supervisor's dispositions, character, and identity. One model is found in Donald Schön's idea of the reflective practitioner.[17] The second model is Palmer's circle of trust.[18]

---

17. Schön, *Reflective Practitioner*; and Schön, *Educating the Reflective Practitioner*.

18. Palmer, *Hidden Wholeness*, 25.

Reflecting on Practice and Circles of Trust

The concept of reflective practice is well-known within the discipline of adult education.[19] Generally, reflective practice is a critical process in which practitioners thoughtfully, carefully, and intentionally reflects upon their own experiences while refining their artistry within their own discipline. In CPE, we speak of this as an action-reflection model of learning. Reflective practice allows for the possibility of learning through experience. It involves the reflecting back on a process or experience even while the process or experience is occurring. In other words, reflective practice involves an ongoing component of formative education.

However, the reflection is not just limited to a program or educational experience. Certainly reflection on these takes place. I would suggest that reflective practice needs to be deeper. It should invite an intentional effort to think not only about the program, but also the issues lying underneath the program, issues involving dispositions, issues raising concerns about character, and issues which embody the identity of the supervisor. Such reflective practice requires that the supervisor looks beyond the obvious content and purpose of the program. The supervisor is thus required to look inward, toward his or her own strengths and weaknesses. Strengths may be quite clear; weakness is not as evident.

Reflective practice on the curriculum planning process can take place in several different ways. The supervisor might journal about his or her experience within the process, drilling down to the issues of the heart; or one might consult with a trusted mentor on the process about what went well and what did not. The supervisor might engage in an intentionally reflective practice with other supervisors as a way of debriefing and giving each other feedback. Feedback is a key element in a reflective practice process. It provides a loop of learning, from the actual planning process back to the supervisor and then back again to the planning process. Schön suggests that this feedback involve a seasoned member of the discipline, a mentor and trusted colleague.

19. Brookfield, *Becoming*; and Mezirow et al., *Fostering Critical Reflection*.

Palmer, it seems, extends the concept of reflective practice to the idea of a circle of trust. He describes a circle of trust as a group of friends and colleagues and peers who have covenanted together to "support rather than supplant the individual's quest for integrity."[20] The purpose of a circle of trust is not to "fix" the person or even give advice. Rather, the purpose is to create a safe space for the person so they can bring, in full honesty, concerns of the heart for reflection. The purpose of a circle of trust is "to make it safe for the soul to show up and offer us its guidance."[21] In its essence, a circle of trust is about a sense of trusted community. The work of circles of trust reminds me of Peter Senge's evocative image of "ruthlessly compassionate" friends.[22]

A circle of trust is not about doing the actual work of the curriculum planning process. It is not about attending to the myriad of details and concerns. A circle of trust is not about following a certain theory of planning. Rather a circle of trust, as Palmer envisions it, is an intentional way of creating time and space for reflection within community and for initiating appreciative inquiry with trusted colleagues.[23] It is an opportunity for the supervisor to bring forth what is within and see ways in which dispositions, character, and identity are embodied. In other words, a circle of trust is more focused on the personhood of the supervisor than the actual planning process itself.

Through reflective practice and a circle of trust, the supervisor has the opportunity to step back, slow down, take a deep breath, and look anew at the many ways his or her values and attitudes and commitments are being lived out. It seems that one of the dangers of a complex and treacherous curriculum planning process is that it is easy for the supervisor to get lost in the details and theories. And by getting lost, the supervisor may allow his or her dispositions, character, and identity to slip into the background where they operate underground and in the dark. An intentional process

20. Palmer, *Hidden Wholeness*, 25.
21. Palmer, *Hidden Wholeness*, 22.
22. Senge, *Fifth Discipline*, 202.
23. Palmer, *Hidden Wholeness*, 72–87.

of reflective practice and use of a circle of trust provides a way for the supervisor's dispositions, character, and identity to stay in the forefront of the curriculum planning process.

Learning occurs in community. Identity is formed within community. Character is experienced in and through communal activities. Dispositions are experienced in and through the give and take of the interdependent relationships found in community. There is no escaping the importance of community in adult learners. Even as one who lives and moves and has his being in solitude, I still know the value of community and relationships. It is a caring community, much like the circle of trust, which calls forth what is within the supervisor even as his or her dispositions, character, and identity embody a walk through life oddly with all the courage, dignity, morality, and ruin that such a walk entails.

12

Symbols and Certification

OVER THE PAST FEW years, I have developed an interest in Native American religion. I have read much about the way of life, the myths, the sun dances, and the sweat lodges. This reading has become a hobby for me and I find myself continually being drawn back to the deep spirituality. I am intrigued by the spirituality of the Native American Indians as they sought purification and visions on the high bluffs and peaks. I am drawn to the role and the power of the medicine man.

Two years ago, as I was preparing to meet the certification committee for associate supervisory status, I did not know what to do with this hobby of mine. I did not know where to place it in my life at that point. I knew that it fit somewhere, but I was at a loss for a way to integrate it into who I was and who I was becoming. In a peer group meeting for supervisors-in-training a couple of months before the committee appearance, we talked about some aspects of Native American religion and spirituality. As we talked, I realized I would make a medicine bundle to take with me to meet the certification committee in Philadelphia.

Medicine bundles were full of power for the Native American Indians, who filled them with symbols of the sacred objects that had been revealed on their vision quests. There might be symbols

Symbols and Certification

of animals, like a bear or a buffalo, or birds, like an eagle or hawk, or people, like an ancient grandfather. All the tangible parts of the vision were gathered together. The bundle then served to remind them that these helpers—the animals or birds or persons—were always nearby and that the helpers were there to give protection and power. The bundles became constant reminders of the vision and the power. In these bundles, then, were the unique symbols of identity and these symbols told much of the story of the individual's life.

I began to work on my medicine bundle. I wanted to find the tangible parts and the symbols which would tell my story and remind me of who I am. My reflections brought me to include these unique symbols: a Moravian medallion to remind me of bone-deep denominational heritage, a cross used in my unofficial ordination in an emergency room during my first year CPE residency, a prayer I wrote to remind myself that deep in my heart of hearts I am a poet, a golf tee to remind me of my easily forgotten playfulness, and an eagle's feather to remind me of my interest in Native American religion and spirituality and the power of symbols. However, as I continued to reflect upon what I was gathering, I could not come up with any symbol that would remind me of my family. The more I thought about it, the more I realized that without this symbol my medicine bundle would not be complete.

About a month before meeting the committee, as I was talking to peers about the symbols I was putting in my medicine bundle, a memory flashed in my mind. I remembered going with my dad, a family doctor, on the winding mountain roads to make house calls when I was a boy. I remembered carrying his medicine bag into the houses for him and watching him talk with these folks, watching him hear their stories, watching him laugh and joke. I saw his compassion and his caring. I saw him go about the healing that came with his medicine bag. I remembered playing with the stethoscope, tongue depressors, and pressure cuffs. I thought back on my life, now as a hospital chaplain, and I remembered what I had learned from him without even realizing it. Here was the symbol that was missing, a symbol of my family and my father. The medicine bundle itself was the symbol. I carried my father's medicine bag on house calls, and now I was carrying my own medicine bundle to meet a committee.

As the weeks wound down and I reflected on my medicine bundle and what it represented about who I am and who I am becoming, I felt whole and centered. I felt powerful. This medicine bundle represented my journey and my call into ministry and into pastoral supervision. This was my vision; this is my vision. There was power in my unique symbols. As I gathered the symbols, the bundle reminded me that no matter what happened in the committee appearance, no one could take from me the feeling of being whole and centered. No one could take from me my vision and my story. My power was in my vision and my story, just as it is for all of us.

My medicine bundle sits on my desk now, reminding me. And I did pass the committee.

13

The Arc of Imagination in Transformative Learning Theory

IN RECENT YEARS THE practice of CPE supervision has widened to include more adult education theory than previously used before. No longer is pastoral supervision anchored solely in a psychiatric model of supervision. Our theory and understanding of how students learn has deepened and has become richer and more varied. Certainly, the great classics from the 1960s and 1970s like Thomas Klink's article "Supervision," Rudolf Ekstein and Robert Wallerstein's *The Teaching and Learning of Psychotherapy,* and Bill Mueller and William Kell's *Coping with Conflict* should continue to be studied and utilized.[1] They are too important to discard. Concepts like cross-grained experience, parallel process, learning problems, problems about learning, and anxiety-avoiding, anxiety-binding, and anxiety-approaching behaviors are foundational to the clinical method of learning.

One of the current adult education theories gaining traction in supervisory practice is that of transformative learning theory. This article will review the basic texts of the theory as they

---

1. Klink, "Supervision," 176–217; Ekstein and Wallerstein, *Teaching and Learning*; and Mueller and Kell, *Coping with Conflict.*

relate to the CPE process, then discuss some of the nuances of the theory, and finally explore how the imagination thickens the clinical learning process.

Overview of Transformative Learning Theory

Transformative learning theory, also known in the adult education literature as transformation theory, is essentially about the process of making meaning. The theory is concerned with how meaning is made out of experiences and, at the same time, how experiences are interpreted to make meaning. In other words, transformative learning theory is about how we, as adults, understand and interpret the many varied experiences that make up our lives and the worlds in which we live and move and have our being. Jack Merizow defines transformative learning as "the process by which we transform our taken-for-granted frames of references (meaning perspectives, habits of mind, mind-sets) to make them more inclusive, discriminating, open, emotionally able to change, and reflective so that they may generate beliefs and opinions that will prove more true or justified to guide action."[2] Patricia Cranton, among others, notes that our taken-for-granted frames of reference are often rigid, formed and shaped by family, social, and cultural expectations. Since we rarely critically question the assumptions that form how we see and experience the world, our frames of reference can be problematic and, therefore, limited and limiting.[3]

We all have particular ways of making meaning of the world and our experiences in it. Life is comfortable when our experiences line up with our expectations. The world is predictable and our footing firm. However, we all know life does not stay comfortable and predictable. Things happen. Our world and our expectations get turned upside down through what transformative learning theory calls *disorienting dilemmas,* events that are epochal and also cumulative over time. These are the experiences that clash

---

2. Mezirow, "Learning to Think," 7–8.
3. Cranton, *Understanding and Promoting,* 36.

The Arc of Imagination in Transformative Learning Theory

with our worldview and assumptions. We are thrown into turmoil. Nothing makes sense. How we understand the world psychologically, socially, and theologically is threatened. We would prefer the world stay the same rather than being made new. The pull of the fleshpots of Egypt is seductive.

Students in CPE experience this kind of turmoil. Encounters with the living human documents often leave them reeling emotionally, spiritually, and theologically. The easy theological world of the academy crashes on the rocks of grief and pain at the bedside. When we are faced with disorienting dilemmas, we have two choices. One is to reject outright the unexpected experience through some sort of coping mechanism like denial, resistance, or repression. We hang on to our worldview at all costs. We defend at all hazards.

The other choice is to take the risk of opening ourselves up to the new experiences and begin the process of critically questioning and reflecting on our unexamined assumptions and beliefs. Can we imagine a new perspective? Can we imagine a new understanding and a new way of being? Can our imagination lead us to more awareness, more acceptance, more hope, more wholeness? Cranton writes, "When people critically examine their habitual expectations, revise them, and act on the revised point of view, transformative learning occurs."[4]

As human beings, we are meaning-seeking and meaning-creating. We live as meaning-hungry creatures. We want our experiences to have meaning; we want our lives to be meaningful. The search for meaning is fundamental to our nature. It is essential and non-negotiable to who we are. The major concepts of transformative learning theory, such as change, meaning, interpretation, and perspective are not new. These concepts are not unique to adult education. They are, in fact, often found in other disciplines. For instance, change and making meaning are essential parts of the psychotherapeutic process.[5] The activity of interpretation plays a major role in the theology and pastoral counseling of John Domi-

---

4. Cranton, *Understanding and Promoting*, 19.
5. Frankl, *Man's Search*; Jung, *Modern Man*; and Stein, *In Midlife*.

nic and Charles Gerkin, respectively.[6] Carrie Doehring looks at the meaning of pastoral care through the lens of modernism and postmodernism.[7] Even traditional Western medicine in all its different forms wrestles with the concept of meaning as it relates to the understanding and interpretation of illness.[8] Finally, the poet Rainer Maria Rilke evokes the making of meaning throughout his body of work.[9]

As a comprehensive theory of adult learning, transformative learning theory is not limited to the bright hallways of the academy. It is applicable—and meaningful—to our clinical method of learning in the swampy, chaotic lowlands of CPE. The challenge for us as CPE supervisors and CPE students is to use our imagination to form and transform our pastoral identities, pastoral competencies, and pastoral functioning. Our hearts are needed as much as our heads.

The Major Texts

The literature on transformative learning theory can be overwhelming. I suggest the best way to get introduced to the theory is to read a text on general adult education and learning. *Learning in Adulthood* by Sharon Merriam, Rosemary Cafferella, and Lisa Baumgartner, published in 2007, is such a text.[10] This is a comprehensive guide to adult learning. It is wide-ranging and expansive. Adult learning is placed in a broad context where issues such as the learning environment, technology, formal and informal programs, and the reality of adult learning are at play. The core of the book focuses on different learning theories and models; for example, the concept of andragogy, self-directed learning, and experiential learning. A student in supervisory CPE can find different theories

    6. Crossan, *Dark Interval*; and Gerkin, *Living Human Document*.
    7. Doehring, *Practice of Pastoral Care*.
    8. Dossey, *Meaning and Medicine*; Duff, *Alchemy of Illness*; Frank, *Wounded Storyteller*; and Mattingly and Garro, *Narrative*.
    9. Rilke, *Book of Hours*.
    10. Merriam et al., *Learning in Adulthood*.

The Arc of Imagination in Transformative Learning Theory

and concepts of adult learning and begin to hone in on a theory for themselves. Be forewarned: There is a lot to grasp.

The chapter of transformative learning sits within the overarching context. Merriam and her colleagues begin by reviewing different perspectives through which the theory can be conceptualized. This is important, for it places the different streams of the theory in theoretical perspective. The student is then challenged to begin his or her process of critical reflection on the theory from both the individual and social perspectives. Next, the major concepts of experience, critical reflection, and development are discussed. Finally, continuing issues and trends are highlighted. Merriam and her colleagues provide a solid, broad overview of transformative learning. One can grasp the concepts of the theory without getting lost. The chapter is clear and succinct. It provides the structure for further reading and will help anchor further understanding.

With the broad overview of the theory in hand, one can then move on to Mezirow's groundbreaking 1991 text, *Transformative Dimensions of Adult Learning*, which is the first major text on the transformative learning theory.[11] Mezirow presents how he understands the dynamics through which we make meaning of our experiences. It is clear that the making of meaning lies at the core of transformative learning theory. Critical reflection here will reveal that Mezirow's conceptualization is based in intellect and rational thought. This text can be quite dense and ponderous in places. For instance, Mezirow gives the reader a heavy dose of philosophy and linguistics as related to adult learning. Thus, this text is heavily weighted toward the scholarly aspects of transformative learning theory. The impact of emotions of the learning process is addressed briefly. The understanding of the affective aspects of transformative learning emerged after the publication of this text. *Transformative Dimensions of Adult Learning* provides a deep, thorough understanding of the theory; it should not be read lightly. In fact, it should not be missed.

---

11. Mezirow, *Transformative Dimensions*.

Mezirow and associates continue the development of the theory in *Learning as Transformation*.[12] This book, published in 2000, came out of the first-ever national conference on transformative learning, which was held in 1998. Here, fifteen scholars wrestle with the developing concepts related to the theory, critiquing and challenging it. The core concepts are discussed as well as areas that need more theoretical attention. Of particular importance is Mezirow's chapter entitled, "Learning to Think Like an Adult."[13] He succinctly summarizes the theory, and again, the process of meaning making is at the forefront. The first section of the book focuses on developing concepts like the constructive-developmental approach, understanding feminist perspectives on learning, and the larger social and ideological implications of the theory. The second section explores the actual practice of transformative learning. Here, one gets to see how the theory unfolds in different settings and contexts. In this way, the theory is thickened and made more nuanced.

In 2006, Patricia Cranton wrote the next major text of transformative learning theory, *Understanding and Promoting Transformative Learning*. Cranton offers a solid description of transformative learning theory and of how such learning is experienced from the learner's perspective, and she gives different strategies for promoting transformative learning. She draws on the most recent scholarship and in doing so pushes the theory forward, especially in the areas of imagination, spirituality, and the significance of affect and emotions in the learning process. Her work, while comprehensive and grounded, is more practical, more readable, and more readily translated into the CPE process that the earlier books mentioned. Mezirow's texts, for example, are located in a more academic and theoretical perspective. A student who delves deeply into Mezirow will certainly have a solid handle on the rational aspects of the theory but will find Cranton's writing more integrated and more holistic. I recommend *Understanding*

---

12. Mezirow et al., *Learning as Transformation*.
13. Mezirow, "Learning to Think," 3–33.

The Arc of Imagination in Transformative Learning Theory

and *Promoting Transformative Learning* as the primary text on the theory.

Finally, all of the theoretical, developmental, research, and current issues in practice are captured in Edward Taylor, Patricia Cranton, and associates' *The Handbook of Transformative Learning*.[14] This volume addresses the theory in-depth and in relation to many different aspects of research and practice. One can read as deeply and widely as desired here. The scope of the scholarship and the different perspectives are impressive. From an overview of the theory to a critique of research on emerging issues such as spirituality in learning, individual differences in learning, and differences in cultural learning, students can find the resources to improve their understanding of transformation and change.

A careful reading of these major texts shows an emphasis on rational thought, critical reflection, and discourse. Although these aspects are important, there is more to transformative learning theory than this rational dimension. The affective dimension of learning also has to be taken into account. Learning in CPE is much more than learning skills from a rational mode. It necessarily involves emotions and affect. This is the only way an effective pastoral identity is forged.

To this end, the student needs to further explore this affective dimension of learning in order to make transformation more complete. Robert Boyd and Gordon Myers offer a different understanding of transformative learning than Mezirow. In fact, they speak of transformative education rather than transformative learning.[15] Boyd and Myers make use of Jungian psychodynamic theory to further develop the sense of a meaningful integrated life. Concepts such as shadow, persona, archetypes, and self are essential. Transformative education is more focused on the wholeness of life rather than a rational understanding of experiences. This is a major difference. An understanding of transformative learning theory is incomplete without a reading of Boyd and Myers's article "Transformative Education." It is that important.

14. Taylor et al., *Handbook*.
15. Boyd and Myers, "Transformative Education," 261–84.

The Care of Souls

Furthermore, the dynamics of grief play a central part in learning, change, and transformation in transformative education. When our worldview is challenged and changed, when our assumptions no longer hold, and when our understandings fail us, the appropriate and necessary response is grief in all its messy manifestations. We are well aware in CPE that grief propels change. We see it at the bedside with patients. We feel it with students as they try to make sense of their experiences. There is no escape. Grief is not rational, cannot be tamed by intellect, and will ultimately have its way with us. Grief is neither rational nor intellectual.

John Dirkx pushed the development of transformative learning further when he introduced the concept of soul into the theory. For Dirkx, soul is not just a theological concept. It is the means through which we make use of imagination, symbols, and emotions in our learning.[16] Dirkx argues that soul leads us to authenticity or, said another way, how we connect head and heart, mind and emotion, darkness and light. By making use of symbols and imagination we open ourselves to learning about ourselves. The process of making meaning centers around the recognition of symbols and use of imagination. For Boyd and Myers and Dirkx, sifting through our emotions is critical to transformative learning. Transformative learning includes both the head and the heart, the intellect and the soul.

As a comprehensive theory of adult learning, transformative learning theory invites the student to wrestle not only with the intellectual foundations but with the more mysterious soul aspects as well. The process of meaning-making involves our whole being. We cannot limit ourselves by relying solely on our rational capabilities. The challenge the theory places before us is to find ways to use our imagination to take us to worlds unknown, to be as open as we are able to embrace the mystery of life, and to honor the journey that is found in the CPE process.

---

16. Dirkx, "Nurturing Soul," 79–88; Dirkx, "Images," 15–16; Dirkx, "Power of Feelings," 63–72; and Dirkx, "Engaging Emotions," 15–26.

The Arc of Imagination in Transformative Learning Theory

The Arc of Imagination

Encounters with the living human documents are often disorienting. We meet persons who are struggling, in pain, or keeping vigil for a loved one. We enter situations where few fear to tread. We are summoned to meet the mystery of chaos with the simple gifts of ourselves, our souls, our imagination. The trite reading of patronizing Scripture verses does nothing to ease grief and pain. More is required. I do not want a pastoral technician to visit me in the hospital; I want a person with soul, who is able to listen, who is able to sit quietly and humbly without having to anxiously cut and run. I want a person who has the imagination to help me find meaning.

How can imagination help us reconfigure the meaning of a disorienting experience? There is no one simple answer. We all have unique imaginations because we are unique persons. To enter into the imaginative world, we are asked to open our eyes to different ways, to open our hearts and let in some pain. We are challenged to look beyond our old, tired assumptions about the world. We are invited to search for new meanings, new symbols, and new hopes. It is only our imagination that allows us to see how God is making all things new even when we would rather hang on to the familiar. Imagination—seeing and feeling larger—helps us to feel the hope, however fleeting, of wholeness.

In CPE, we ask students to trust the process. We ask them to trust us as supervisors, to trust the group, and to trust themselves. I often feel that by saying, "Trust the process," we are encouraging students to imagine the process, that is, to imagine the journey one step at a time towards a faraway, elusive promised land. We need our imagination to search for meaning, to create meaning, and to satisfy our hunger for meaning. Jungian psychotherapist and author James Hollis puts it succinctly: "Meaning makes a great many things endurable—perhaps everything."[17] How else will we stumble through the pain we find at the bedside unless we can somehow summon our imagination as a way to meaning?

---

17. Hollis, *Archetypal Imagination*, 13.

I recall a middle-aged woman I visited one time. She had terminal cancer; she was dying. She was angry because the cancer had been initially misdiagnosed. She had every good reason to be angry. The first thing she said to me when I entered her darkened room was: What is heaven like? Of course, I stammered. I had no answer. So I asked her what she thought. Somehow this led to conversation about her life, her daughter, her illness, and now her dying. Over the next several weeks as she was in and out of the hospital, our conversations always included her question.

On her last admission, she told me that she had to move in with her elderly parents because she needed them to take care of her. She spoke of her mother cooking her favorite meals and how all the familiar smells would fill the house. She would sit in the kitchen as her mother cooked. Her father would take her outside in her wheelchair to sit under her favorite tree and watch the birds in the garden. I asked her how all this made her feel. She thought for a moment, then softly said it made her feel safe. She felt deeply loved amidst all the memories of her home. She felt at peace. Then, somewhere from my imagination, a gift perhaps, I replied that maybe this is what heaven is like. We sat quietly for a long while as she drifted off to sleep.

That was our last conversation. She died that night. The meaning of home was the meaning of heaven for her. She made her meaning. I would like to think that somehow I helped.

The arc of imagination invites us to see more, to feel more, to be more, to live larger so that our pastoral care will be more soulful. Of course, the meanings we make through our imagination come by way of our histories, our complexes, our narratives, our limits. Meanings are contested. There is not just one right answer. Imagination helps us look beyond the narrow confines of our assumptions. Jung says, "In the same way that the body needs food, and not just any kind of food but only that which suits it, the psyche needs to know the meaning of its existence—not just any meaning, but the meaning of those images and ideas which reflect its nature and which originate in the unconscious."[18]

18. Jung, "Philosophical Tree," para. 476; and Burns, *Paths to Transformation*, 54.

The Arc of Imagination in Transformative Learning Theory

Learning and finding meaning in CPE is not easy. In fact, the process can be quite disorienting, unlike any other learning experience the student may have had. The process of becoming a self-aware pastoral caregiver is more complex than learning a multiplication table or learning how to operate a machine. To move into the necessary affective dimension of transformative learning, students are invited—and challenged—to surrender. That is, students are asked to be willing to learn to surrender and likewise, to surrender to learn. Said another way, students are given the opportunity to learn to let go and to let go in order to learn. In the CPE process, we are invited—and challenged—to let go of our unexamined assumptions and ways of understanding the world and to then imagine a process that offers a new way of being in the world. Of course, the letting go of our assumptions never happens without a fight. We hang on to what we know; paradoxically, learning in CPE propels us toward what we do not know. Learning in the CPE asks us to make better use of our imagination.

It is our imagination that helps is live into our grief and pain rather than run away from them. It is our imagination that enables us to, however tentatively, hold on to our darkness as well as our light, believing that God is in both, that when God calls us, the call embraces both darkness and light. It is our imagination that helps us see beyond our shadow and flaws, so we can live into who we are and who we hope to be. It is our imagination that allows us to surrender the tight hold that shame claims on our lives. To think, see, and feel larger than shame means we are to surrender our need to hide. Instead of hiding, we are challenged to take the imaginative risk to be seen, to be heard, and to be known. In doing so, we confess honestly our failures and brokenness and can then freely receive the absolution of knowing we are forgiven and accepted. Imagination helps us find the mercy we all need.

Learning in CPE is difficult because the setting is difficult. Students are thrown into the fire where there are no easy, sure answers. The pain is real. The grief is real. The disorientation is real. Uncertainty and not-knowing echo through the halls of the hospital, in seminars, and in supervision. Imagination is required more

The Care of Souls

than ever in the face of what Hollis calls the Triple As: ambiguity, ambivalence, and anxiety.[19] Nonetheless, as difficult as the learning process is in CPE, it is equally as transformative and life-changing for both students and supervisors. Transformative learning theory gives the most accurate and compelling understanding of the learning process. It is important to remember, however, that the magic, miracle, and mystery of transformation are quietly found in our imagination. Imagination makes meaning possible. Imagination makes transformation possible.

---

19. Hollis, *Archetypal Imagination*, 63.

14

The Dream and the Gift

SEVERAL YEARS AGO, I had a dream about Granny. The dream came to me during a difficult point in my life. I was growing up and leaving home in a new and different way. It was an awful, painful time. In this dream, Granny brought me comfort and understanding. She always did.

My granny was one of those special mothers who graced my life and helped fill up some of my emptiness. She had soft white hair with a bluish tint, a slow walk, and eyes that spoke of unsaid words of hardship and dignity and love. Granny had a countenance and a way about her that said things would be all right. Her hugs were easy, her bosom was one of comfort, her lap one of safety. There was a gentleness about her that somehow understood all my temper tantrums and all my lost and lonely feelings. Granny could always make me feel better. She let me into her life in unspeakable ways.

When a thunderstorm appeared on the horizon, Granny would ever so quietly take a chair from the kitchen and go into our small guest bathroom where there were no windows. There she would sit, all safe, as the thunder rumbled, the lightning flashed, and the rain swept down. Granny was terribly afraid of thunderstorms, and yet, she was unafraid of mine.

When I reached my teenage years, I pushed her away. All of a sudden, I was now too grown up for her. Her perfume was too strong, her hugs too tight. Her bosom was uncomfortable, her lap restraining. I needed space and room and freedom. Granny then gave me that. She died when I was 17. It was hard to cry at her funeral. I did not know what to feel. Even now, I am not sure what all I lost that day.

I grew into adulthood. My life, my loves, and my vocation were unfolding. I became aware of a slow but steady trickle of revelation about my childhood. Throughout my life, I have received many gifts and many hungers have been met. But I still needed to mourn, for there were still things not received and hungers not met. At times, I felt like an angry adolescent; at other times, like a small boy howling in my tantrums. My Great Sadness, as Pat Conroy calls it, was real.

And so I grieved. Then one night Granny came to me in a dream. I don't remember the context of it or if any words were spoken. But words were not necessary. I simply remember the vividness in which she came to me. She was *there* with the blue-tinted hair, the gentleness, the bosom. Granny taught me in this dream that there are always things we do not receive and hungers that are not met, but no matter, it was all right. I was still loved and accepted and forgiven. Granny brought me comfort in a difficult time for she blessed my growing up and leaving home. I did not push her away this time, not in this dream. I felt wrapped up in her love. Granny still understood my storms and she was not afraid of them.

The next morning I told my wife about the dream. She listened intently and simply said, "It must have been good to see her again." And I cried.

Granny came to me in a dream and in her special way, let me know it is not wrong or bad to hunger or to feel empty or to grow up and leave home. We are all that way in our heart of hearts. In spite of hungers and our emptiness and maybe because of them, we are still loved, accepted, and forgiven. I am still loved, accepted, and forgiven.

That is the gift.

Bibliography

ACPE. *Standards of the Association for Clinical Pastoral Education.* Decatur, GA: Association for Clinical Pastoral Education, 2010.
Bond, D. Stephenson. *The Archetype of Renewal: Psychological Reflections on the Aging, Death, and Rebirth of the King.* Toronto: Inner City, 2003.
Boyd, Robert, and Gordon Myers. "Transformative Education." *International Journal of Lifelong Education* 7 (1988) 261–84.
Brookfield, Stephen. *Becoming a Critically Reflective Teacher.* San Francisco: Jossey-Bass, 1995.
———. *Understanding and Facilitating Adult Learning.* San Francisco: Jossey-Bass, 1986.
Brueggemann, Walter. "The Costly Loss of Lament." In *The Psalms and the Life of Faith,* edited by Patrick Miller, 98–111. Minneapolis: Fortress, 1995.
———. "From Hurt to Joy, From Death to Life." In *The Psalms and the Life of Faith,* edited by Patrick Miller, 67–83. Minneapolis: Fortress, 1995.
———. *The Message of the Psalms: A Theological Commentary.* Minneapolis: Augsburg, 1984.
———. *Praying the Psalms.* Winoa, MN: St. Mary's, 1986.
———. "Psalms and the Life of Faith: A Suggested Typology of Function." In *The Psalms and the Life of Faith,* edited by Patrick Miller, 3–32. Minneapolis: Fortress, 1995.
———. "The Psalms as Prayer." In *The Psalms and the Life of Faith,* edited by Patrick Miller, 33–66. Minneapolis: Fortress, 1995.
———. *Reverberations of Faith: A Theological Handbook of Old Testament Themes.* Louisville: Westminster John Knox, 2002.
———. *Spirituality and the Psalms.* Minneapolis: Fortress, 2002.
Burns, Kate. *Paths to Transformation: From Initiation to Liberation.* Asheville, NC: Chiron, 2015.
Cabot, Richard, and Russell Dicks. *The Art of Ministering to the Sick.* New York: MacMillan, 1947.
Caffarella, Rosemary. *Planning Programs for Adult Learners: A Practical Guide for Educators, Trainers, and Staff Developers.* San Francisco: Jossey-Bass, 2001.

Bibliography

Campbell, Joseph. *The Hero with a Thousand Faces*. Princeton: Princeton University Press, 1986.

Capps, Donald. "Psalms, Pastoral Use of." In *The Dictionary of Pastoral Care and Counseling*, edited by Rodney Hunter, 969–70. Nashville: Abingdon, 1990.

Cervero, Ronald, and Arthur Wilson. *Planning Responsibly for Adult Education: A Guide to Negotiating Power and Interests*. San Francisco: Jossey-Bass, 1994.

Covey, Stephen R. *The Seven Habits of Highly Effective People: Restoring the Character Ethic*. New York: Simon and Schuster, 1989.

Cranton, Patricia. "Fostering Authentic Relationships in the Transformative Classroom." *New Directions for Adult and Continuing Education* 109 (2003) 5–13.

———. "A Jungian Perspective on Transformative Learning." In *Proceedings of the Fifth International Conference on Transformative Learning*, edited by Colleen Wiessner et al., 120–25. New York: Teachers College of Columbia University, 2003.

———. *Understanding and Promoting Transformative Learning: A Guide for Educators of Adults*. San Francisco: Jossey-Bass, 2006.

Cranton, Patricia, and Carusetta, Ellen. "Developing Authenticity as a Transformative Process." *Journal of Transformative Education* 2 (2004) 276–93.

Crossan, John Dominic. *The Dark Interval: Towards a Theology of Story*. Sonoma, CA: Polebridge, 1988.

Daloz, Laurent. *Effective Teaching and Mentoring: Realizing the Transformational Power of Adult Learning Experiences*. San Francisco: Jossey-Bass, 1986.

de Laszlo, Violet, ed. *The Basic Writings of C. G. Jung*. Princeton: Princeton University Press, 1990.

Dirkx, John. "Engaging Emotions in Adult Learning: A Jungian Perspective on Emotion and Transformative Learning." *New Directions for Adult and Continuing Education* 109 (2006) 15–26.

———. "Images, Transformative Learning and the Work of Soul." *Adult Learning* 12 (2001) 15–16.

———. "Nurturing Soul in Adult Learning." *New Directions for Adult and Continuing Education* 74 (1997) 79–88.

———. "The Power of Feelings: Emotion, Imagination, and the Construction of Meanings in Adult Learning." *New Directions for Adult and Continuing Education* 89 (2001) 63–72.

Dirkx, John, et al. "Musings and Reflections of the Meaning, Context and Process of Transformative Learning: A Dialogue Between John M. Dirkx and Jack Mezirow." *Journal of Transformative Education* 4 (2006) 123–39.

Doehring, Carrie. *The Practice of Pastoral Care: A Postmodern Approach*. Louisville: Westminster John Knox, 2006.

Dombkowski Hopkins, Denise. *Journey Through the Psalms*. rev. and exp. St. Louis: Chalice, 1998.

Dossey, Larry. *Meaning and Medicine*. New York: Bantam, 1991.

Bibliography

Duff, Kat. *The Alchemy of Illness*. New York: Bell Tower, 1993.
Edinger, Edward F. *The Sacred Psyche: A Psychological Approach to the Psalms*. Toronto: Inner City, 2004.
Ekstein, Rudolph, and Robert Wallerstein. *The Teaching and Learning of Psychotherapy*. New York: International Universities Press, 1972.
Endres, John. "Psalms and Spirituality in the 21st Century." *Interpretation: A Journal of Bible and Theology* 56 (2002) 143–54.
Frank, Arthur. *The Wounded Storyteller: Body, Illness, and Ethics*. Chicago: University of Chicago Press, 1984.
Frankl, Victor. *Man's Search for Meaning: An Introduction to Logotherapy*. New York: Pocket Books, 1984.
Friedman, Edwin H. *Generation to Generation: Family Process in Church and Synagogue*. The Guilford Family Therapy Series. New York: Guilford, 1985.
Gerkin, Charles V. *The Living Human Document: Pastoral Counseling in a Hermeneutical Mode*. Nashville: Abingdon, 1984.
Grabove, Valerie. "The Many Facets of Transformative Learning Theory and Practice." *New Directions for Adult and Continuing Education* 74 (1997) 89–96.
Gunkel, Hermann. *The Psalms*. Philadelphia: Fortress, 1967.
Hemenway, Joan. *Inside the Circle: A Historical and Practical Inquiry Concerning Process Groups in Clinical Pastoral Education*. Decatur: The Journal of Pastoral Care, 1996.
Hersey, Paul, and Kenneth Blanchard. *Management of Organizational Behavior: Utilizing Human Resources*. Englewood Cliff: Prentice Hall, 1972.
Hillman, James. *The Force of Character and the Lasting Life*. New York: Random, 1999.
———. *Insearch: Psychology and Religion*. Dallas: Spring, 1990.
———. *The Soul's Code: In Search of Character and Calling*. New York: Random, 1996.
Hollis, James. *The Archetypal Imagination*. College Station, TX: Texas A&M University Press, 2000.
———. *Creating a Life: Finding Your Individual Path*. Studies in Jungian Psychology by Jungian Analysts. Toronto: Inner City, 2001.
Housden, Roger. *Ten Poems to Change Your Life*. New York: Harmony, 2001.
Jinkins, Michael. *In the House of the Lord: Inhabiting the Psalms of Lament*. Collegeville, MN: Liturgical, 1998.
Johnson, David, and Frank Johnson. *Joining Together: Group Theory and Group Skills*. Boston: Allyn and Bacon, 2000.
Jones, Logan C. "Baptism by Fire in Clinical Pastoral Education: The Theory and Practice of Learning the Art of Pastoral Care Through Verbatims," *Reflective Practice* 7 (2006) 125–42.
Jung, Carl. *Modern Man in Search of a Soul*. New York: Taylor & Francis, 2001.
———. "The Philosophical Tree." In *The Collected Works of C.G. Jung*, vol 13, edited by Gerhard Adler and R. F. C. Hull. Princeton: Princeton University Press, 1967.

Bibliography

Klink, Thomas. "Supervision." *Theological Education* 3 (1966) 176–217.

Knowles, Malcolm, and Hulda Knowles. *Introduction to Group Dynamics*. New York: Association, 1972.

Mattingly, Cheryl, and Linda C. Garro, eds. *Narrative and the Cultural Construction of Illness and Healing*. Berkeley: University of California Press, 2000.

Meade, Michael. *Fate and Destiny: The Two Agreements of the Soul*. Seattle: GreenFire, 2010.

Mennecke, Brian E., et al. "The Implications of Group Development and History for Group Support System Theory and Practice." *Small Group Research* 23 (1992) 524–72.

Merriam, Sharan B., et al. *Learning in Adulthood: A Comprehensive Guide*. San Francisco: Jossey-Bass, 2007.

Mezirow, Jack. "A Critical Theory of Adult Learning and Education." *Adult Education* 32 (1981) 3–24.

———. *Education for Perspective Transformation: Women's Reentry Programs in Community Colleges*. New York: Center for Adult Education, Columbia University Teachers College, 1975.

———. "Learning to Think Like an Adult: Core Concepts of Transformation Theory." In *Learning as Transformation: Critical Perspectives on a Theory in Progress*, edited by Jack Mezirow et al., 3–33. San Francisco: Jossey-Bass, 2000.

———. "Perspective Transformation." *Adult Education* 28 (1978) 100–110.

———. *Transformative Dimensions of Adult Learning*. San Francisco: Jossey-Bass, 1993.

———. "Transformative Learning as Discourse." *Journal of Transformative Education* 1 (2003) 58–63.

———. "Transformative Learning: Theory to Practice." *New Directions for Adult and Continuing Education* 74 (1997) 5–12.

———. "Understanding Transformation Theory." *Adult Education Quarterly* 44 (1994) 222–32.

Mezirow, Jack, et al. *Fostering Critical Reflection in Adulthood: A Guide to Transformative and Emancipatory Learning*. San Francisco: Jossey-Bass, 1990.

———. *Learning as Transformation: Critical Perspectives on a Theory in Progress*. San Francisco: Jossey-Bass, 2000.

Mowinckel, Sigmund. *The Psalms in Israel's Worship*. Nashville: Abingdon, 1962.

Mueller, William, and Bill Kell. *Coping with Conflict: Supervising Counselors and Psychotherapists*. Englewood Cliffs: Prentice-Hall, 1972.

Murphy, Roland. "The Faith of the Psalmist." *Interpretation: A Journal of Bible and Theology* 34 (1980) 229–35.

Napier, Rodney W., and Matti K. Gershenfeld. *Groups, Theory and Experience*. Boston: Houghton Mifflin, 1999.

Norris, Kathleen. *The Cloister Walk*. New York: Riverhead, 1996.

Bibliography

Nouwen, Henri. "Case-Recording in Pastoral Education." *Journal of the Academy of Parish Clergy* 4 (1974) 1–11.

Palmer, Parker. *The Courage to Teach: Exploring the Inner Landscape of a Teacher's Life.* San Francisco: Jossey-Bass, 1998.

———. *A Hidden Wholeness: The Journey Toward an Undivided Life.* San Francisco: Jossey-Bass, 2004.

Peck, Scott. *The Different Drum: Community Making and Peace.* New York: Touchstone, 1998.

Pleins, J. David. *The Psalms: Songs of Tragedy, Hope, and Justice.* Maryknoll, NY: Orbis, 1993.

Rilke, Rainer Maria. *Rilke's Book of Hours.* Translated by Anita Barrows and Joanna Macy. New York: Riverhead, 1996.

Schön, Donald. *Educating the Reflective Practitioner: Toward a New Design for Teaching and Learning in the Professions.* San Francisco: Jossey-Bass, 1987.

———. *The Reflective Practitioner: How Professionals Think in Action.* New York: Basic, 1983.

Scott, Sue M. "The Grieving Soul in the Transformation Process." *New Directions for Adult and Continuing Education* 74 (1997) 89–96.

Senge, Peter. *The Fifth Discipline: The Art and Practice of the Learning Organization.* New York: Doubleday, 1990.

Shepperd, Gerald. "Theology and the Book of Psalms." *Interpretation: A Journal of Bible and Theology* 46 (1992) 46 14–55.

Sork, Thomas. "Planning Educational Programs." In *The Handbook of Adult and Continuing Education,* edited by Arthur L. Wilson and Elisabeth R. Hayes, 171–90. San Francisco: Jossey-Bass, 2000.

Stein, Murray. *In Midlife: A Jungian Perspective.* Dallas: Spring, 1983.

———. *The Principle of Individuation: Toward the Development of Human Consciousness.* Wilmette, IL: Chiron, 2006.

Taylor, Edward. "Making Meaning of the Varied and Contested Perspectives of Transformative Learning." Paper presented at the Proceedings of the Sixth International Conference on Transformative Learning. Lansing, MI: Michigan State University 2005.

Taylor, Edward, et al. *The Handbook of Transformative Learning: Theory, Research, and Practice.* San Francisco: Jossey-Bass, 2012.

Vella, Jane. *Training Through Dialogue: Promoting Effective Learning and Change.* San Francisco: Jossey-Bass, 1995.

Westermann, Claus. *Praise and Lament in the Psalms.* Atlanta: John Knox 1981.

———. "The Role of the Lament in the Theology of the Old Testament." *Interpretation: A Journal of Bible and Theology* 28 (1974) 20–38.

Wiessner, Colleen Aalsburg. Personal communication, 2005.

Yalom, Irving D. *The Theory and Practice of Group Psychotherapy.* New York: Basic, 1995.